VANCE CLAYTON THROUGH THE YEARS

by Michael E Stockham

Typeset in Iowan Old Style

Editing, design and publishing by UK Book Publishing

UK Book Publishing is a trading name of Consilience Media

www.ukbookpublishing.com

ISBN: 978-1-910223-30-7

CONTENTS

CONTENTS

Preface by the author

Having moved to the North East back in the early 1970's to take up new employment in the region and being a 'southerner' I knew little of the rich and diverse nature of entertainment in North East clubland and its availability (at that time) at nominal cost. I consequently became a member of several local Working Men's Club and Institute Union (CIU) clubs and was soon frequenting Newcastle night clubs and other entertainment venues in the wider region. As a result and as a lover of 50's & 60's music before long I became aware of *The Vance Clayton Trio* and appreciated their combined talents and in particular the voice of their front man and vocalist Brian Leonard otherwise known as Vance Clayton.

As the years went by the workingmen's club and entertainment scene changed significantly - in part probably attributable to the paying public's changing taste, their drinking habits altering and the cost of entertainment substantially increasing. Larger pubs, where entertainment used to be regularly staged, and many workingmen's clubs closed and indeed continue to close for lots of reasons including loss of revenue, mismanagement and most recently the smoking ban. My individual circumstances also altered through personal and employment commitments and I hadn't seen or indeed heard of Vance Clayton for many years.

Before my retirement back in 1996 I took on the

role of Secretary for a former treat fund (now a registered Charity) and started by the miners at a local colliery over 100 years earlier which provides treats for the children and seniors of the village. These include an annual, all expenses paid day out to Seahouses on the Northumberland coast for the seniors in which the charity, in addition to providing coach travel and a 4 course midday meal, also lays on entertainment during the afternoon. Some years ago Jack Livingstone, an organist & vocalist from the Borders who provided that entertainment for many years, retired and I was asked to find a replacement.

It so happens that some months before the annual trip that year my wife and I were invited to a couple's Golden Wedding anniversary party and were delighted to find out that *The Vance Clayton Duo* was providing the entertainment. To cut a long story short I got chatting to Brian Leonard during a break and found out that at that time he and Davey Herron, his drummer, played at The Benedictine Club in Cramlington on a Sunday night, The Ship at Monkseaton on a Tuesday night and The Seahorse at Blyth on a Wednesday as well as private engagements – either as a duo or Brian, alone, as an organist & vocalist when Davey is unavailable. The Charity Chairman Les Shiell & I paid a couple of visits to The Seahorse to listen to them and in Committee later decided that Brian would be an ideal replacement for our annual trip to Seahouses. A role he continues to perform for the Charity.

Therefore, having established that Vance Clayton was 'still in business', my wife and I became regulars at The Ship and The Seahorse and got to know the duo quite well. Well enough to be invited by them to some of their other engagements one of which was to a Sunday night Christmas show that Brian did for Mel Harmison at his pub The Anglers Arms in Sheepwash Northumberland. The Anglers Arms has excellent accommodation attached and along with Brian & his lovely wife Helen, my wife and I stayed overnight and over breakfast on the Monday morning we got talking and Brian & Helen started to recall some of their experiences during his long career in the entertainment business. I said to Brian that he should write them down as they would make a good book and indeed could form the basis of his autobiography. In his usual modest and unpretentious way he replied that he wasn't capable of doing that and as a result I suggested that I would be prepared to assist him. He readily agreed.

He & I therefore embarked on a metaphorical journey through the years and into Brian's past during which I learned that he is actually two 'different' people which those close to him will appreciate. One is the man - Brian Leonard - the husband, father, grandfather and friend and the other - Vance Clayton - the entertainer. Through countless hours of conversation in his and their company and dictated 'ramblings' on a digital voice recorder neither he nor Helen have held back and have told their stories as it was and is, warts and all, unabridged and definitely not glamorised. This book is therefore most definitely not politically correct in today's terms but by the same token it is not intended to shock the reader, offend anyone living nor to besmirch the memory of those no longer with us.

Although by nature quiet, shy and unassuming Brian doesn't suffer fools gladly, has never forgotten his working class roots and is greatly loved and respected by his family. His three sons all commenting that as well as being their father he's their best friend too. Although now over seventy years 'young' Brian remains an outstanding vocalist and according to many of his peers in the entertainment world can still out-perform many of the industry's highest paid artistes. I therefore sincerely hope that I have done justice to both the man and the performer because they both deserve it and I also trust that you will get as much enjoyment out of the book as you read it as I have in researching and writing it.

Please note that it is both Brian's & my expressed wish that any revenue and royalties from the sale of the book will be donated to the registered UK charity Epilepsy Action, the working name of the British Epilepsy Association, and the choice of Brian & Helen.

Enjoy!

Michael E Stockham

VANCE CLAYTON
THROUGH THE YEARS

April 1942

April 1942 and World War 2 had been raging for two and a half years having started on the 3rd September 1939 when Neville Chamberlain, Britain's Prime Minister, declared war on Germany. Millions of people around the world were enduring great hardship and none more so than those in London which suffered tremendous damage and loss of life in the period of the Blitz between September 1940 and May 1941 when more than one million homes were destroyed or damaged and nearly 20,000 people were killed. On the 15th April 1942 the strategically important Mediterranean island of Malta was awarded the George Cross by King George VI to *'bear witness to the heroism and devotion of its people'* during the siege by the air forces and navies of Fascist Italy and Nazi Germany which its inhabitants had been suffering since mid-1940. The siege finally ended in November of the same year.

The North East of England like other heavily industrialised regions of the UK was also a prime objective for the German Luftwaffe and April 1942 had the inhabitants of Consett and the surrounding area in the north west of County Durham under constant threat of their own Blitz as the Germans targeted incendiary and high explosive bombs at the Consett Iron Company in the town. The Company operated iron and steel works, collieries and brick making facilities in the area so crucial to the nation's war effort and employed around 12,000 people at that time.

In Bridgehill close to the town a couple of its residents, William Henry Leonard and his wife Ruby Gray (née Stafford) were anxiously looking forward to the birth of their first child. William (better known as Harry), aged 28 who worked in the ironworks and Ruby, aged 27 had married in 1940. Fortunately none of the bombs hit the property where they lived because Ruby was afraid to leave the house for the safety of the air raid shelter.

The baby was born on Wednesday 29th April 1942 and Brian Cecil Leonard uttered his first sounds. Little did his mother and father know that his dulcet tones and musical prowess would, in just a few years time, entertain many thousands of music lovers and until this very day, over 70 years on, people still pay to listen to him play and sing. Shortly after Brian was born his father Harry was called up for military service and along with his brother Charlie joined the British Army and was eventually posted to Africa.

Ironically Brian's mother Ruby herself had been born just 3 months after the First World War started on 4th August 1914 and was just a year old when her father George Robert Stafford enlisted. She was barely 2½ years old when he was wounded in France and tragically died of his injuries.

Goodness only knows therefore what Ruby must have been thinking when Brian's dad Harry went off to war so soon after their baby was born knowing that her mother had been widowed as a young woman with two very small children just 25 years earlier. Nonetheless history was fortunately not to be repeated and Harry returned safely.

George Robert Stafford was born in Hull East Yorkshire in February 1892 the son of Cecil Montague & Emma Stafford (née Roberts). His birth mother died in 1903 when they were living in Bramley West Yorkshire and his father married Marian Louise née Fildes in 1904 in Leeds West Yorkshire. By 1911 the family, comprising George aged 19, his father (a travelling photographer), his step-mother, brother Cecil aged 15 and half-brother Reginald aged 6, half-sisters Marian Louise aged 5, Constance aged 3 and Marjorie Irene aged 2 had moved to 12, Wilson Street Dunston on Tyne and George was working as an invoice clerk for a hay & corn merchant.

He later became an insurance agent for the Liverpool Victoria Insurance Company and met and married Elizabeth Cowan née Gray on 30th April 1913 in Dunston Parish Church. Their first child was a daughter Ruby Gray Stafford (later to become Brian Leonard's mother) who was born on 8th November 1914. As a family they lived in Embleton Cottage, 23 Spoor Street Dunston on Tyne.

George enlisted in the Durham Light Infantry as Private 31608 on 10th December 1915 and was placed on Reserve from 11th December 1915 until 10th April 1916 when he was Home posted. On enlistment, his records show that he was 5ft 8ins tall, weighed 10st 2lbs with a 36½ ins chest (39½ ins expanded) and was declared fit for general service.

George was made an Acting Lance Corporal (unpaid) on 10th June 1916 and paid on 1st July 1916. On the 1st September 1916 he was transferred to 10th (Service) Battalion York & Lancaster Regiment as Lance Corporal 39860. On 18th December 1916 10th Battalion were transferred to the British Expeditionary Force (BEF) as part of the 37th Division and on the same day sailed from Folkestone in Kent to Boulogne for service in France.

On 28th February 1917 his wife Lizzie gave birth to a son Cecil Montague Stafford.

37th Division of which the 10th Battalion were a part were involved in the Battle of Arras on the Western Front in 1917 when from 9 April to 16 May 1917, British, Canadian, New Zealand, Newfoundland and Australian troops attacked German defences near the French city of Arras. On the 23rd April 1917, in the Second Battle of the (river) Scarpe, the British launched an assault east from Wancourt towards Vis-en-Artois and secured the village of Guémappe. In the face of strong German resistance the decision was taken not to push forward and on the 24th April the attack was called off.

George Stafford was a machine gunner and sustained a compound fracture of the right femur on 24th April 1917 and was treated by members of the 48th Field Ambulance (48th FA) of the Royal Army Medical Corps. 48th Field Ambulance served with the 16th (Irish) Division which was established by the Irish Command in September 1914, as part of Kitchener's Second New Army. They moved to England and into barracks in Aldershot later that month. In June 1915 they transferred to 37th Division and proceeded to France in July, the division concentrating near Tilques. In 1917 they fought in The First Battle of the Scarpe, including the capture of Monchy-le-Preux, and in April 1917 in the Second Battle of the Scarpe.

George was taken to No. 4 General Hospital in Dannes-Camiers by 48th FA. Dannes-Camiers was the huge base depot of the British Army in France, just north of Étaples and inland from the dunes on the English Channel coast and close to what is now the elegant and fashionable resort of Le Touquet – Paris Plage and playground of rich Parisians. Camiers camp was also the base depot of the Machine Gun Corps in France and was a particularly notorious base camp for those on their way to or back from the front. Under atrocious conditions, both raw recruits and battle-weary veterans were subjected to intensive training in gas warfare and bayonet drill and long sessions of marching at the double across the dunes. After two weeks many of the wounded would rather return to the front with unhealed wounds than remain at Étaples. In the words of Olave, Lady

Baden-Powell, the wife of Robert Baden-Powell the founder of Scouting and Girl Guides, it was *'a dirty, loathsome, smelly town'*.

A compound fracture of the femur is even with today's medical advances a very serious injury and needs to be operated on as soon as possible. The femur is the longest, heaviest and by most measures the strongest bone in the human body and to break it requires substantial force or sustained trauma. In wartime compound fractures were and indeed still are often incurred as a result of direct gunfire or shrapnel from a bomb or shell explosion and such injuries in World War One were very frequent. Complications such as haemorrhage, wound infection, internal organ damage and acute respiratory distress were common and the chance of survival from such trauma during that war was only 20%.

Although mortally wounded George dictated a poignant letter to his wife Lizzie on 26th April 1917 from his hospital bed. It read as follows:

26/4/1917

My own darling you will no doubt [have] *received a felted postcard which I sent two days ago. You will not altogether be surprised to hear that I have been wounded. I am at present in C. C. S. Hospital* [Casualty Clearing Station Hospital] *and expect to go down the base very shortly. From there I may be sent on to England as my hands are practically useless. I am getting someone to write this for me owing to having my hands packed with plaster of Paris this last 3 days. Try not to worry little girl and perhaps things may be better shortly and we shall see each other again very soon shortly. Best love to Ruby, Monty and yourself.*

Ever your own George xxxxxx

xxxxxx

Given the severity of his injuries, not surprisingly, George Robert Stafford died of his wounds 10 days later on 4th May 1917. He is buried in the Commonwealth War Graves cemetery in Étaples France and the commemoration reads as follows:

STAFFORD, Lce. Cpl. George Robert 39860. 10th Bn. York and Lancaster Regt. Died of wounds 4th May 1917. Age 26. Son of Mr & Mrs Cecil M Stafford of Hull; husband of E C Stafford of 24 Spoor Street Dunston-on-Tyne. Native of Hull. XVIII. H. 16A.

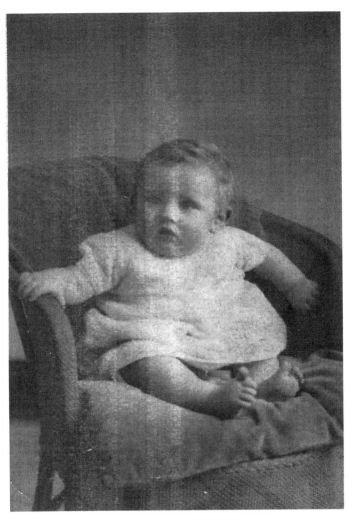

BRIAN CECIL LEONARD

**L/CPL GEORGE ROBERT STAFFORD,
WIFE LIZZIE & DAUGHTER RUBY 1916**

In late September 1917 George's widow Lizzie received articles belonging to him including letters, photos, cards, insurance pocket book, religious book, wallet, tobacco pouch and cap badge. In November 1917 she received confirmation that she had been awarded a pension of 22/11d (one pound, 2 shillings and 11 pence) a week for her and the two children to be paid with effect from 12th November 1917 – a full six months after her husband's death. In today's currency that equates to £1.15 but with inflation would now represent £78.42 per week.

The Early Years

As a toddler Brian was given a photograph of his father by his mother and on Harry's return from Africa at the end of the war Brian refused to acknowledge that this man was his real dad because he was so brown – showing him the photo and saying *"That's MY daddy"*. It took Brian some time to get used to him!

Like so many children at that time with fathers away serving their country Brian was spoilt rotten by his Mam and immediately after the war and the return of the menfolk some discipline had to be enacted. Brian recalls being put in his Uncle Charlie's kit bag and hung up on the back door hook when he was naughty - which he often was!

When he was 3½ years old the Leonards moved from Consett to Dunston, on the south bank of the River Tyne to No. 9 Wellington Road – a terraced house owned by Grandma Lizzie Stafford which they shared with his mother's brother Cecil Stafford, his wife Judy and their two children Colin and Joan. The Staffords had the back room and back bedroom, the Leonards had the front room and front bedroom and the kitchen was shared. The nettie (or toilet) was in the back yard and they shared the use of a tin bath which also hung there.

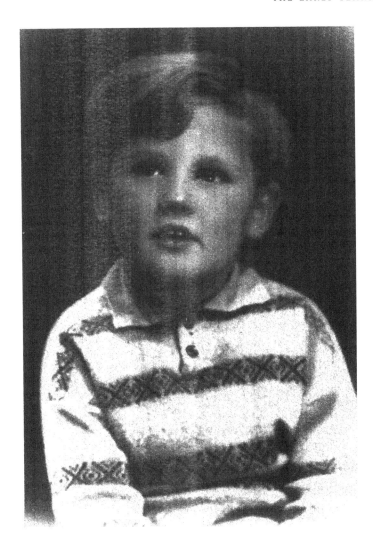

BUDDING MUSICIAN

The neighbouring city of Newcastle upon Tyne had many entertainment venues including the Moss Empire Palace in Newgate Street (known locally as the Empire) which staged pantomimes and Brian was taken there by his Mam in 1945, full of bronchitis and a snotty nose. Nevertheless this didn't deter the little budding musician, during a lull in the programme, from standing on his seat and announcing to the compere that he too could sing. *"Go ahead"* replied the compere and Brian launched into his rendition of 'Mighty Like A Rose':

MIGHTY LIKE A ROSE

Sweetest little fellow, everybody knows;
Don't know what to call him but he's mighty like a rose!
Lookin' at his mammy with eyes so shiny blue,
Makes you think that heaven is comin' close to you.

When he's there a-sleepin' in his little place,
Think I see the angels looking thro' the lace.
When the dark is falling, when the shadows creep,
Then they come on tip-toe to kiss him in his sleep.

Sweetest little fellow, everybody knows,
Don't know what to call him but he's mighty like a rose!
Lookin' at his mammy with eyes so shiny blue,
Makes you think that heaven is comin' close to you.

Not exactly Paul Robeson nor Frank Sinatra but apparently Brian got a great ovation and plenty of sweets.

In April 1946 the first of Brian's two sisters, Sandra was born and in May 1949 Kathleen completed the family. His Uncle Cecil and Aunt Judy had another son named Geoffrey about this time. The Leonard family lived in No.9 until 1951 when Brian was 9 years old and they moved into a three bed-roomed council house farther away from the river and close to the main A1 road at No. 141 Beech Drive Dunston.

The immediate post war period was tough for working class families, money was in short supply and some aspects of food rationing which had been introduced soon after the war started became even stricter. Although bread rationing was lifted in 1948, clothes in 1949, petrol in 1950 sweet and sugar rationing continued until 1953 and it wasn't until the 4th July 1954 that saw the end of meat and all food rationing in the UK. Brian's father was working for Dunston Council as a refuse collector and his mother would often joke that they shopped in bins (*Binns was a department store with branches across the North East of England*).

It is a generally accepted fact that there was greater community spirit in those days than exists today when doors were left unlocked and neighbours regularly got together and shared whatever they had. Brian's Mam Ruby and her friend, Esther Johnson, from across the street in Beech Drive were no exceptions and would get together every Friday and prepare spaghetti bolognese. Ruby prepared the mince and as an Italian lady Esther made the pasta. The families would sit together and devour the banquet.

In October 1947 Esther Johnson (née De Luca) and her husband Alan had a son and called him Brian. Brian Johnson, like Brian Leonard, also grew up with a penchant for music performing in scout gang shows and singing in the local choir but quickly became attracted to rock and roll. He joined the Newcastle based band called *USA* in 1972 and they soon changed their name to the far more appropriate *Geordie* and went on to have a couple of Top 20 hits with 'All Because Of You' and 'Can You Do It'. The band eventually went out of fashion and disbanded in 1976 only to reform in early 1980 at Brian Johnson's request.

Bon Scott, the lead singer of the Australian hard rock band *AC/DC*, died in February 1980 and although the remaining members considered disbanding, Angus Young the group's guitarist and co-founder recalled that Bon Scott had seen *Geordie* and admired Brian Johnson's voice, likening it to Bon's idol Little Richard. In March 1980 Brian Johnson was invited to audition for the lead singer role in *AC/DC* and on 1st April 1980 he was selected as Bon Scott's replacement and where he still is today.

Esther Johnson, Brian's Mam, in her broken English, would regularly say to Ruby, Brian Leonard's Mam

"Your Brian - he got a lovely voice – my Brian he shout!"

The Leonard family were a lovely, lovely family according to another one of their next door neighbours in Beech Drive - Jeff Burdon. Jeff now lives in Orlando, Florida in the USA and remembers that they had a warm, caring and open home that was always full of friends. Harry and Ruby Leonard were a contradictory couple according to him – Ruby was softly spoken, a little reserved and wouldn't upset anyone and Jeff's late mother loved having her as a friend. Harry on the other hand was gregarious, funny and candid and always spoke his mind.

Jeff recalls an incident in about 1960 or 1961 when as usual and as a friend, he would be helping Brian Leonard with electrics and the wiring up of Brian's audio gear which he had spread around the house between kitchen and living room. One day Jeff was in the kitchen stripping the insulation from the ends of the wires in a cable (with his teeth as usual) and the other end with the 3 pin plug top on it lay on the living room floor. Brian walked past it, picked it up and plugged it into a socket nearly blowing Jeff's brains out! Not so humorous at the time but Jeff saw the funny side of it – later!

They were and remain good friends, exchanging visits over the years one of which Brian recalls when he and his wife Helen had taken a cruise in Florida and took the opportunity to spend a few days with Jeff and his wife. During the visit they met a friend of

Jeff's, a film director called Pat Williamson who lived near the exclusive and private Orange Tree Golf Club, which is situated close to Orlando's central business district. Although in his eighties at the time Pat was a member and still played there and he invited Brian & Jeff for an all expenses paid day's golf which they gratefully accepted.

The idiom *'it's a small world'* is appropriately demonstrated by an incident that Jeff recollects when his friend Pat Williamson told him that, with his ailments, he was having difficulty getting in and out of his Jaguar and had decided to purchase a Bentley and asked Jeff to accompany him to the car showroom. When the salesman heard Jeff's Geordie accent he told him that he talked just like a musician friend of his who lived some 70 miles down the road. Jeff said *"That'll be Brian Johnson from AC/DC"* and the salesman, somewhat taken aback replied *"How do you know that?"*. Jeff explained that Brian Johnson was a neighbour when they both lived in Dunston in the UK. Well the guy didn't really believe him and asked how he would know Jeff was telling the truth. Jeff replied *"Two things – one; we both bought motor cycles from the Post Office when they were finished with them and two - he would know another neighbour from Dunston - Brian Leonard also known as Vance Clayton."* The salesman disappeared and when he came back he told Jeff that he had phoned Brian Johnson who had indeed remembered and asked *"Is that old bugger Brian still singing?"*

Jeff's abiding memory of Brian Leonard in their younger days is that he always had 'drop-dead' gorgeous girlfriends, one after another. In Jeff's words *"It was a bit like playing Blackjack – Brian kept saying 'twist' until he met Helen and then it was 'stick'. Lovely fella, lovely lady!"*

Brian Cecil Leonard attended Dunston Hill Secondary Modern School and admits that he wasn't a very bright pupil but greatly enjoyed music. As a schoolboy he was also a chorister at the Church of England, Christ Church in Dunston.

By any stretch of the imagination the Leonard family were not well off financially but nevertheless enjoyed themselves and after church on a Sunday they would all meet up and entertain by singing and playing musical instruments. As a bin man Brian's dad Harry would bring home all sorts of things that other people had discarded including musical instruments such as saxophones, clarinets, guitars, ukuleles and banjos and someone in the family would manage to play most of them. Harry and his Uncle Charlie played guitars, mandolins and ukuleles and an old Aunt played the zither and the family would sit around singing along.

Uncle Charlie Leonard and his wife Freda had two boys Trevor and Dennis. Dennis took after his father and also played the guitar, mandolin and ukulele and sang. He went on to perform in the clubs as a solo artist and also with two girls as a trio for about 4½ years. However his singing career eventually came to end when his wife Sally gave birth to a baby they named Joseph. Nevertheless and to the present day he often helps his cousin Brian with his computer and sings when Brian invites members of the audience to get up and entertain.

Charlie's sister Annie and her husband Billy Bramley also had two sons, Leonard and Stuart and Leonard, who shared the same birthday as Brian (29th April although 5 years older), also played the guitar. He and Brian were great friends and although suffering from terminal cancer he was determined to be present when Brian & Helen hosted a birthday bash for Brian's 70th & Helen's 65th birthdays in April 2012 and Brian sang 'Happy Birthday' to him. Sadly Leonard passed away just 2 weeks later.

Brian was therefore born into a large and established musical family and introduced to music by that family and principally by his father and Uncle Charlie who taught him a few chords on the guitar. At the age of 13 Brian got up in front of the assembled school and accompanied himself on a guitar singing the country and western song 'The Man From Laramie' made popular in the UK by Jimmy Young. The Man from Laramie became Brian's nickname throughout the rest of his school days.

He formed a close friendship at school with Jimmy Allan who also lived in Beech Drive Dunston. Jimmy was just a little lad and a bit of a sickly child and seemingly always had a snotty nose, didn't like school and would feign illness at the drop of a hat. *"Please Miss I'm not well at all"* Jimmy would plead with the teacher in the afternoon. *"Anyone live near Jimmy?"* came the teacher's reply. *"Aye me Miss, we're neighbours"* Brian would call out! *"Take him home then Brian for the rest of the afternoon and make sure he's alright"* The pair of them would then leg-it to Banky fields next to Carrs Bank in Dunston where they would hide and have a smoke! Jimmy didn't like sports very much either at school and would seek ways to avoid P E lessons by feigning illness and claiming to be unable to vault the horse or play a part in other gymnastic exercises. Whilst he would be excused actually participating he would have to get the apparatus out of the cupboard including the vaulting horse. One day the P E lesson arrived and Jimmy asked Brian to help him shift the vaulting horse and suggested they hide under it – shades of the 1950 Second World War film The Wooden Horse – and Brian agreed. They climbed under the horse and whilst sat in the dark listening to their classmates jumping over and crashing into the wooden box Jimmy lit up a cigarette! Within a couple of minutes smoke began to seep through the seams of the wooden structure and the P E teacher pulled the top off and found them both crouched inside. Needless to say a few strokes of the cane followed along with lines and detention. That was Jimmy!

Like Brian he also played the guitar and went on to a successful musical career with John McGarry and

Stevie Baxter when they formed a group called *This, That and The Other*. John McGarry would later change his stage name to John Garrimore when he went solo as a comedian. Brian Leonard & Jimmy Allan still keep in touch.

Determined to further his love of music and the guitar Brian took a paper round at Jarrons, the newsagent in Dunston and saved to buy a Framus Black Rose guitar from Jeavons the music store in Percy Street, Newcastle.

The paper round took in the aforementioned Carrs Bank (named after Sir Ralph Carr-Ellison who owned large areas of land in Dunston, Whickham & Swalwell) which was the steepest hill in Dunston and a real *'cardiac arrest'* according to Brian. His sister Kathleen was only 5 years old at the time but would help her brother deliver the papers. She did the farthest deliveries while Brian had a smoke and if she complained her brother would tell her she'd get no sweets or be thrown in the pig pen at the farm on the way back down the hill. Brian built a scooter to which he fastened the heavy paper bag and would push it up the hill which took about an hour. With Kathleen in the front and Brian steering from the rear the journey back down the farm track to Jarrons shop took only 3 minutes.

THE CHORISTER

SCHOOL PHOTO
BRIAN 2ND LEFT BACK ROW & JIMMY ALLAN IN CENTRE

CARRS BANK DUNSTON 1959

Start of music career

Brian left school aged 14½ and got a day job with
Michell Bearings in Scotswood Road Newcastle upon
Tyne as a cost clerk. Michell Bearings Limited was
established in Newcastle in 1920 and remains today
the world's premier designer and manufacturer of
hydrodynamic bearings. In the evenings he would
join up with his cousin Colin Stafford, who played
the guitar, and with Brian on piano they played at
The Bay Horse public house in Whickham. They got
£2 each with which they bought 20 tabs (cigarettes)
and got drunk on Black Velvets – Guinness (stout
beer) and white wine.

Brian also started singing for a cancer charity with
a female impersonator called Harry English and
a group of dancers. As well as singing Brian also
played the guitar. This lasted for a few months until
he performed at a concert at Newcastle University
for Cancer Research which comprised several other
acts. The main group that night was *Eddie Silver* (real
name Edward John George Sivell) *and The Railroaders*
(a five piece band) with their backing group of female
vocalists *The Ladybirds*. These were followed on stage
by a dancing troupe and a couple of singers. Whilst
they were performing Brian struck up a conversation
with two of *The Railroaders* guitarists and when it
came to his turn on stage he sang 'He's Got The
Whole World In His Hands' (later made popular by
Laurie London) and 'Honeycomb' (by Marty Wilde)
and the two guitarists got up on stage and backed

him. He later discovered that the two guitarists were in fact Hank Marvin & Bruce Welch who of course went on to form *The Shadows* with Jet Harris and Tony Meehan, replacing *The Drifters* as the backing band for (Sir) Cliff Richard.

BRIAN WITH COUSIN COLIN STAFFORD

In the audience that night were a group of lads from
Dunston some of whom Brian knew from school
and they told him they had formed a six piece band
called *The Gators* and invited him to join them playing
guitar and singing. The band members included
the brothers Brian & Will Pears, Dave Shipley, Ian
Watson, Jim Hall and Michael Lant. Brian agreed
and before long in 1957 they were playing clubs and
pubs all over the North East of England and mainly
in Ashington where there were 28 clubs alone so they
seldom had to double up in one club during the year.

BRIAN WITH BRUCE WELCH LATER IN THEIR CAREERS

One night they were booked to appear at a club in
Ashington but just down the road at another club the
group hadn't turned up. So *The Gators* divided and 4
members stayed at one club and the other 3 went to

the club down the road.

Every weekend they would hire a bus from Swalwell near Dunston and all their friends and fans would pay two shillings (10p) and travel to whichever venue the band were performing and Brian's dad Harry would frequently join the trip and connect with the locals. One such trip was to the Grand Street Club in Ashington where the band had a particularly successful night and as usual Harry got himself well-served (drunk) by bragging to the locals about his son. At the end of the night the bus was loaded and they set off back to Dunston. They got as far as Bedlington and Brian noticed that his dad wasn't on board. *"Oh no"* he said *"We've left the old bugger behind!"* The bus was turned round and went back to Ashington but Harry was nowhere to be found. On the way back to Dunston the bus was travelling through the Teams at Gateshead when someone spotted Brian's dad walking along the street. Having missed the trip bus his drinking pals in Ashington had put him on a service bus and because Brian had turned round in Bedlington Harry got back before the rest. *"Fine bunch of mates you are leaving me in Ashington!"* exclaimed Harry.

The Caroll Levis Discovery Show

Caroll Richard Levis was a Canadian talent scout, impresario and radio and television personality who moved to England in 1935 and joined the BBC. In the 1950's he toured the country with a talent competition for young people called *The Caroll Levis Discovery Show*. The shows were hosted by the gorgeous Jackie Collins, the then less well known and younger sister of the actress and film star Joan Collins. Jackie was expelled from school aged 15 but went on to become a bestselling novelist. One such talent show was held in the Sunderland Empire and Brian and *The Gators* entered but came second to a group called *The Dallas Boys* (arguably Britain's first boy band). Needless to say that Brian and his mates enjoyed their short time with Miss Collins – following her around *"like dogs in heat"* according to Brian!

Not to be deterred by their disappointment in Sunderland the lads entered again when the show came to the Newcastle Empire in 1958 and Brian sang 'Move It' which was top of the charts as performed by *Cliff Richard And The Drifters*. They won the competition by a country mile and were awarded a prize which was a week filming the show at the BBC Television studios in Birmingham with *The Dallas Boys, Billy Fontaine* and other singers and comics who had won shows around the country.

They were a great success singing two songs by the Canadian group *The Diamonds* – 'Little Darlin'' and 'Walking Along'. Although they won many plaudits and loads of fan mail unfortunately, shortly afterwards, four of the band got called up for National Service and that was the end of *The Gators*.

Vance Clayton

At about that time Brian decided to join the Territorial Army as a military policeman at the TA Centre, Debdon Gardens in Heaton, Newcastle upon Tyne where his uncle George Bradley was a Sergeant Major. Brian recalls that his uncle treated him pretty badly and particularly on the parade ground where he would often refer to Brian's drill performance as being like a *'bag of shit'* and didn't give his nephew the lickings of a dog. Yet when Brian was invited to play the piano in the Sergeant's mess he was as nice as pie! When off duty and questioned by Brian over a pint George told him that if he had treated him better than the other lads they would have resented him for it. Brian served for two years in the TA and attended one two week camp down in Sherwood Forest in Nottingham.

Following the demise of *The Gators* Brian joined a concert party called the *Denbry Show* playing piano and singing as well as backing other singers including Amy Bryden, a songstress likewise hailing from Beech Drive in Dunston and a Frank Sinatra type singer. Also in the show was a magician from Blaydon called *Tom Scott the Wizard*.

THE GATORS – BRIAN PLAYING THE
COVETED FRAMUS BLACK ROSE GUITAR ON
THE CARROLL LEVIS DISCOVERY SHOW

Brian spent a year with the show around the clubs
and pubs doing 'go as you pleases' for £2 prizes. He
did a Jerry Lee Lewis act on the piano with 'Great
Balls Of Fire'. At that time the Smith Brothers had
a pub in Felling called The Ship and ran 'go as you
please' competitions with 'pick a prize' winnings
including packets of razor blades and flower vases!
The Five Smith Bros had been a big band in the 1950s
and early 1960s and were regulars on the BBC
Regional Variety radio show Wot Cheor Geordie
where they opened their act with *"Hello, hello, hello,
hello, h-e-l-l-o* (each brother singing and going higher
up the scale and the last one holding a much longer
note) *This is Mr & Mrs Smith's five little boys, who are
saying to you...."* They appeared on the Royal Variety

35

Performance shows in 1950 and 1955.

Brian's day job continued at Michell Bearings where a lad from the factory floor called Tony Carruthers worked and asked him if he would be interested in joining the group he played in called *The Strangers*. Brian met up with the other lads and they hit it off and it was soon 'goodbye Denbry Show' and 'on the road with *The Strangers*'. They gave Brian the stage name Johnny Silver. After a year or so as *Johnny Silver and The Strangers* they decided to change their name as there were other groups called *The Strangers*.

Andy Muat, the lead guitarist used an echo chamber called an Echolette and the band decided to call the group *The Echolettes* but Brian as lead vocals needed a name.

At the time they were working the Clayton ballroom in Bedlington and Keith Patterson the group's drummer felt that Clayton would make a good surname so all they needed was a first name. Duffy Cliff the group's bass player was reading a western comic and recited the sentence - *"Vance road into town and shot the sheriff"*. *"I like the sound of that, that's a great name"* said Brian and *Vance Clayton* was born!

JOHNNY SILVER & THE STRANGERS

KEITH PATTERSON (DRUMS)
DUFFY CLIFF (BASS) ANDY MUAT (LEAD)
TONY CARRUTHERS (RHYTHM) & BRIAN (VOCALS)

They worked at the Clayton ballroom every Friday night for the best part of a year and on one such night a group called *Shane Fenton & The Fentones* were also playing there. In those early days of the 1960s, they were an unknown teenage band who recorded a demo tape and mailed it in to the BBC with the hope of being picked to appear on TV. While awaiting a reply from the BBC, the band's 17-year-old singer *Shane Fenton* (born John Theakstone), died from the effects of the rheumatic fever he had suffered in childhood. The rest of the band, guitarists Jerry

37

Wilcox and Mick Hay, bassist William "Bonny" Oliver and drummer Bobby Elliott had decided to break up. However they unexpectedly received a letter from the BBC inviting them to go to London to audition for a programme. The late John Theakstone's mother asked the band to stay together, and to keep its name, in honour of her son's memory. Bernard Jewry, who was a roadie with the group at the time, was asked to become the new Shane Fenton. The combo had a handful of hits in the UK Singles Chart basing their sound on that of *The Shadows*. Bernard Jewry disappeared from the spotlight for a decade after the break-up of the Fentones, working in music management and performing at small venues with his wife Iris Caldwell, the sister of Rory Storm of *Rory Storm and The Hurricanes* whose drummer was Ringo Starr. During the early 1970s, however, Jewry acquired a new persona, Alvin Stardust, as he successfully cashed in on the glam rock bandwagon. His debut hit was 'My Coo Ca Choo' in 1973. He was diagnosed with prostate cancer in 2013 and sadly passed away in October 2014 aged 72 just before his first album for some 30 years was due to be released.

The five piece band *Vance Clayton and The Echolettes* toured the North East playing in pubs and clubs and at dances. One such gig in 1961 was a regular weekly dance at Burradon Youth Club in North Tyneside where a 14 year old lad called Davey Watson was so impressed by the way Brian dressed in tight pants and a silver lamé jacket that he was inspired to start a career of his own in the music business. He copied the style and went on to play in groups around the region and later formed a trio with his wife Carol Anne and Derek 'Dec' Jackson, the guitarist from *Geordie*; and later a duo with his wife called *Double Trouble*. Davey & Carole Ann and Dec all continue to ply their respective talents around the remaining pubs and clubs still booking entertainment today.

A regular in the audience at Burradon was an attractive 14 year old young lady from High Pit in Cramlington called Helen Nesbitt who thought *Vance Clayton* was a bighead and didn't like him at all – that was of course to change in the years to come. In any event at that time Brian was engaged to an aspiring beauty queen called Jackie Turnbull.

In the early 60's Brian met a friend from Gateshead by the name of Eric Smith who was a motor mechanic and he took on the job of keeping the band's vehicles on the road. He opened a garage in Swalwell called E & M Motors (named after himself and his wife Miriam) and he acted as the band's road manager as they chased around the North East doing doubles in Consett and Darlington on the same night. Strong as a horse he was nicknamed Hercules as he would have the gear stripped down and in the van before the lads had their suits off! Smithy and his wife were and remain Brian & Helen's good friends and would often holiday together abroad.

The Vance Clayton Trio

1963 and Brian and The Echolettes took time off for a camping holiday in Scotland where they ended up in Oban on the west coast and on the Saturday night they went to a dance where they saw a band playing called *The Burnettes*.

That band was originally formed in Folkestone Kent, in 1962, from two local Kent bands, Neil Landon from *Pat and The Cheetahs* (Neil's real name was Pat Cahill) and Pete Kircher, Noel Redding, and Bob Hiscocks, from *The Lonely Ones*. They toured England with a couple of weeks in Scotland including Wick in the far north, Oban on the west coast and Aberdeen in the east. In January 1964 they were booked to play the Storyville Club in Frankfurt, Germany. The owner of the club, Jon Marshall, insisted they had five in the band, so as they were playing for a couple of weeks in the Manchester area, they auditioned and enlisted the very capable Kevin Lang (from Manchester) on bass. Incidentally, Kevin's brother Bob Lang was the bass player with *Wayne Fontana and The Mindbenders*.

Noel Redding was chosen by Chas Chandler to join Jimi Hendrix in 1966 at the inception of *The Experience* and he was the first band member and switched from playing guitar to bass, Mitch Mitchell joined as drummer. Noel's playing style was distinguished by his use of a pick as opposed to plucking the strings. He left the band in 1969 and joined up again with Neil Landon and formed *Fat Mattress* who supported the *Jimi Hendrix Experience* on tour.

Pete Kircher joined *Honeybus* in 1967 and in the early 70s joined the band *Shanghai* with Mick Green from *Johnny Kidd and The Pirates* and playing as a session drummer on the album 'The World's Not Big Enough' with John Du Cann and produced by *Status Quo*'s guitarist Francis Rossi. This in turn eventually led to Pete being invited to join *Status Quo* as their drummer when John Coghlan left the group in 1981.

The Burnettes had a two-manual (2 keyboards) organ called a Bird Duplex and the sound completely knocked Brian Leonard and the lads out when they heard it. Andy Muat & Keith Patterson asked Brian if he fancied downsizing the five piece band to a trio and getting an organ. That Saturday night out in Oban would therefore prove to be a turning point in the band's development and Brian's career and ultimately lead to the birth of the *Vance Clayton Trio*.

When they returned to the North East Brian checked out the price of the two-manual organ and found out it cost around £2,000 and certainly well out of the band's reach. By this time Brian had left his day job at Michell Bearings Limited and got another as assistant buyer for a firm called Adams Powell Equipment on the Team Valley and was one day talking to the Deputy Managing Director who was leaving the company to work in the USA. He told

Brian that he had heard Brian was quite a competent musician and that he had a rather nice piano he wouldn't be taking to the States and wanted to see it go to a good home. Brian accepted and the Deputy MD arranged for a driver and company vehicle to have it delivered to Beech Drive Dunston where Brian was still living with his parents and two sisters.

Brian was later sat at his desk when the phone rang and he took a call from his mother who was ringing from a callbox at the end of their street. The conversation went something like this: *"Our Brian there's a wagon at our house with the biggest harp you've ever seen and the man says it's for you! What do you want me to do?"* she pleaded.

"Don't worry Mam just leave it - I'm on my way!" Brian hastily replied, jumped on his motorbike and drove home.

His mother wasn't far wrong in her assessment as the wooden frame had been stripped from the piano but when reassembled in the family's dining room it turned out to be a Bechstein Concert Grand Piano and in Brian's words *'the most beautiful piano he'd ever seen and certainly the best he'd ever played'*. The only problem was the Leonard family had to eat off it because there was no space for any other furniture in the room! Brian played the grand piano for a few months before visiting the City Music Stores in Newcastle where he invited the proprietor to buy the piano. They agreed a price which roughly covered the cost of purchasing the coveted Bird Duplex organ. The band downsized and that was the beginning of *The Vance Clayton Trio* comprising Andy Muat on guitar, Keith Patterson on drums and Brian on keyboards and vocals.

With his day job at Adams Powell, smoking and doing clubs and pubs every night - burning the candle at both ends were to take their toll on Brian's health. One day his Mam found him lying at the bottom of the stairs and phoned for an ambulance and Brian was rushed to Whickham Hospital and subsequently Shotley Bridge Hospital in Consett where he was diagnosed with pneumothorax (collapsed lung) and underwent surgery to patch up his right lung. He was in hospital for a couple of weeks during which time his mother never missed a visit, two buses every night all the way to Consett and then on to Shotley. She was, as Brian recalls, a Saint. After getting out of hospital he spent two weeks convalescing and then back to the graft. It took him a while to learn to sing from his diaphragm as his left lung had to do the job of two.

ON MY WAY MAM

Whilst performing at Shiremoor Working Men's Club Brian had met a guy named George Spowart who went on to get the band work at other venues and drove the group's transport. He looked after them and they spent a lot of time at his place at Moor Side in Shiremoor. George worked at a clothing factory in Newcastle and that was where Brian's future wife also worked.

Swan Hunter, the world famous Ship Design and Shipbuilding Company based in Wallsend on Tyneside, was to be Brian Leonard's next employer where he was engaged for the next two years as an assistant buyer. On his own admission Brian didn't claim to have worked there but rather to have attended because most of his time was spent writing songs and preparing play lists for the trio's gigs.

In addition to the hundreds of working men's clubs

and public houses in the North East of England in the 60's and 70's providing entertainment, many 7 nights a week, there were also a selection of more 'up market' establishments and nightclubs. In the mid to late 60s in particular Newcastle had an exciting night life which, outside of London, was possibly the best for music, dancing, wining and dining and had about a dozen such establishments a lot of which were also casinos. All offered late night entertainment acts many of which were recording and television stars of the day. South Shields & Sunderland had Latino and Wetheralls, in Middlesbrough there was Contessa and Marimba and Tito's & La Bamba could be found in Stockton and Darlington and Newcastle featured The Cavendish, La Dolce Vita, Club A'Gogo and Greys Club among others.

Shortly after acquiring the sought-after Bird Duplex organ the trio found work at the Club A'Gogo which was opened and owned by Mike Jeffrey, a former Londoner, who went on to manage *The Animals* and later to co-manage Jimi Hendrix with Chas Chandler. After a fire at his Marimba coffee bar on High Bridge and dwindling attendances at his two jazz venues – the New Orleans in Melbourne Street and the Downbeat Club in Carliol Square in Newcastle – Mike Jeffrey established Club A'Gogo on the top floor of a building in Percy Street. It was in the same block as The Handyside Arcade but all long since demolished and built on as part of the Eldon Garden Shopping complex. The club was divided into two distinct sections – the licensed Jazz Lounge and the unlicensed Young Set providing music for teenagers under the legal age for drinking.

Alan Price, later to link up with Eric Burdon and form *The Animals* and in 1965 *The Alan Price Set*, regularly performed in the Jazz Lounge of Club A'Gogo with his first group called *The Alan Price Rhythm and Blues Combo*. Alan would often call in on Brian, Andy Muat and Keith Patterson in the other section of the club and play on the Bird Duplex. One night Brian, Andy & Keith were invited by Alan to the Jazz Lounge to listen to an impromptu jam session with a singer called 'Long John' Baldry with Reggie Dwight on piano and a shy young lad by the name of Rod Stewart on guitar. On another occasion Alan Price invited Brian and the lads to see Jimi Hendrix play in the Jazz Lounge of the Club A'Gogo.

'Long John' Baldry and Rod Stewart eventually got together with Geoff Bradford (an accomplished Blues guitarist) and formed a Rhythm & Blues (R & B) group called *Long John Baldry and His Hoochie Coochie Men* in 1964 which in 1965 became *Steampacket*. In 1966 Reg Dwight on keyboards joined forces with Baldry and Elton Dean on saxophone as the R & B group *Bluesology*. Reg Dwight would of course become Elton John, a stage name he put together by combining Elton from Elton Dean and John from 'Long John' Baldry.

The *Vance Clayton Trio* also secured contract work at La Dolce Vita, The Cavendish, The Vine Grill and

Wetheralls in the North East as well as similar night spots in Yorkshire and Lancashire as the support act for the top performers. This would entail performing either the 10pm or midnight spot depending on when the top of the bill was on stage. For one such week Brian and the lads were engaged to support the duo Jet Harris and Tony Meehan, both former members of *The Shadows*, with Harris unusually playing Fender Bass VI guitar as the lead instrument and Meehan on drums. The duo had had hit singles in 1963 with 'Diamonds' (UK No.1), 'Scarlett O'Hara' (UK No.2) and 'Applejack' (UK No.4). On the Monday of that particular week Brian, Andy and Keith did the 10 o'clock spot at The Cavendish and made their way to Wetheralls in Sunderland to follow Jet Harris and Tony Meehan for the midnight performance. It transpired that Jet Harris had shown up for the 10pm performance as 'drunk as a skunk' and couldn't perform. On the Tuesday the performance times were reversed and the *Vance Clayton Trio* arrived at Wetheralls for the 10 o'clock show only to find out that Jet Harris & Tony Meehan had been paid off and Brian & the lads had been promoted from support act to top of the bill.

Following his acrimonious departure from *The Shadows* in 1962 Jet (Terence) Harris was suffering deep depression and had turned to alcohol purportedly as a result of his then wife's alleged affair with Cliff Richard. He subsequently split with Tony Meehan in September 1963. After some 30 years of heavy drinking he finally acknowledged his alcoholism and sought help. He was awarded an MBE in 2010 for his outstanding services to music and died of cancer in March 2011. Tony Meehan briefly played again with *The Shadows* when Brian Bennett was in hospital and later became an artists and repertoire (A&R) man for Decca. A devout Roman Catholic he died in November 2005.

As Brian remembers it was no problem being top of the bill in the North East where they had a following anyway but hardly anyone knew of them in places like Sheffield and Manchester where the other contracted venues were. As he readily admits for example the top billing of Bob Monkhouse one week, followed by Tommy Cooper on week 2 to *Vance Clayton* the next week was a tough call for the lads as well as the night clubbers. Nevertheless the series went well and was a great experience.

At The Vine Grill in Sunderland the *Vance Clayton Trio* of Brian, Andy Muat and Keith Patterson secured a contract for Fridays, Saturdays & Sundays doing 12 midnight to 2 am and after performing at workingmen's clubs in the evening. Local Sunderland entertainers such as the much loved comedian Bobby Knoxall in his singing days and singer Johnny Longstaff were regulars at The Vine Grill and Brian recalls a struggling, and in the artist's own words "starving singer" Gerry Dorsey, recovering from the very serious illness tuberculosis, literally 'sang for his supper' backed by the trio. Gerry Dorsey, following an unlikely name change to Engelbert Humperdinck by his and the super star Tom Jones' then manager Gordon Mills, became one of the biggest earning performers of the 1960s and 1970's after the recording of 'Release Me' in 1967.

Andy Muat remembers that whilst the trio were rehearsing at the Vine Grill one afternoon George Watson who ran the restaurant had thrown *The Rolling Stones* out when they had called in for a meal describing them as "five scruffy looking bastards" - the 'infamous' five being Mick Jagger, Keith Richards, Brian Jones, Bill Wyman & Charlie Watts. They were actually playing the Sunderland Odeon in March 1965 as part of their very first British Tour along with *The Hollies, Dave Berry & The Cruisers, Goldie & The Gingerbreads, The Checkmates* and *The Conrads* with Johnny Ball as compere. One of Andy's claims-to-fame is that he also recalls *The Rolling Stones* coming back early that evening and asking him if they could borrow a guitar amplifier as one of theirs had packed in – he duly loaned them one and was consequently thanked by them!

Marriage & family

The Pioneer Club in Annitsford Northumberland proved to be a venue that Brian would never forget. The trio were performing there one Sunday night in 1963 when Brian got his eye on Helen Nesbitt who was dancing with her friend Carol and he said to Andy Muat that he quite fancied the lass with the pink hair and big tits! Andy went over to the girls during the interval and subsequently Brian was introduced to Helen. Things developed romantically from there (as they do) and two years later on the 23rd January 1965 Brian and Helen were married in the Old Chapel in Church Street Cramlington Northumberland – later to be converted to an Italian Restaurant called San Lorenzo. Their reception was held in High Pit Social Club Cramlington where Brian, along with his pals, the resident duo, Johnny Ashcroft on the organ and Tommy Dowson on drums, had performed and would continue to perform until its closure at the turn of the new millennium.

Tommy would later become a close friend and golfing partner of Brian including trips to Portugal and Majorca. When Brian & Helen were living in Eastfield Green in Cramlington Tommy lived opposite them in a flat and on one occasion the pair of them were booked to perform at a charity event and in the afternoon, prior to the show, were scheduled to play golf. The morning arrived and Tommy went to see Brian and said that although they were supposed to play golf that afternoon he had forgotten that he was booked to have a vasectomy that morning in Blyth and asked if Brian would accompany him as he was somewhat nervous. Brian agreed but said that he needed to be back to play golf in the afternoon. So off they went and after having the procedure Tommy came out saying that he felt ok and suggested that he caddied for Brian that afternoon. Before playing the two of them had a couple of pints and a bite to eat and probably with the *Dutch* courage Tommy said that he felt great and that he would actually play. Despite Brian's advice he played and as they were changing to leave Tommy again reported that he felt great and well enough to play the drums at the charity show that night. Once again and in spite of warnings from Brian not to overdo things he played the drums all night.

At about half past six the next morning Brian got a telephone call from Tommy pleading with him to *"Come over quick and have a look at these man Clayton-please!!!"* Brian got dressed and went over to Tommy's flat to find him in agony with his testicles swollen up and in Brian's words *"as big as case balls!"* Brian told him that he had warned him not to over exert himself by playing golf and then the drums all night. *"It wasn't just that man I brought a lass back and had me leg over!"* exclaimed Tommy.

A 550-seater social club, High Pit was referred to locally as the Palladium of the North and a regular port of call for some of the country's top performers including Lulu, Tony Christie, Showaddywaddy, Frankie Vaughan and Bernard Manning to name but a few. It was at High Pit Club that Brian would develop a close relationship with the then concert chairman, the late George MacLean who along with Hughie & Ian Turner would eventually become Brian's agent at Wansbeck Theatrical Agency.

Helen & Brian honeymooned in Blackpool where they took in all the shows on the three piers (North, Central & South) along the Golden Mile and meeting acts some of whom Brian would later perform with and become good friends. They lived in Granny Lizzie Stafford's house in Wellington Road Dunston where Brian had lived as a kid. The grandmother had offered to sell it to them for £500 but Brian refused the offer because it had an outside 'netty' (toilet) and no bathroom. However before long Harry, Brian's dad and Helen's dad Kit (Christopher) Nesbitt put a bath in the kitchen with an Ascot water heater. It took a 'month of Sundays' to fill the bath but when you're young and in love it didn't really matter.

Some 18 months after they were married Brian & Helen were delighted when Helen gave birth to the first of their three sons Tony, prematurely, in Queen Elizabeth hospital in Gateshead on the 30th July 1966. Coincidentally the day that England won the Jules Rimet trophy (World Cup) beating West Germany 4-2 at Wembley.

Although employed and as a part time musician/

entertainer Brian was unable to secure a mortgage but the lack of satisfactory toilet and bathing facilities was an inconvenience so with a young family he and Helen decided to rent a bungalow in Whickham a few miles west of Gateshead. A complete luxury compared with 9, Wellington Road Dunston.

THE HAPPY COUPLE

HARRY & RUBY LEONARD - BRIAN &
HELEN - BELLE & KIT NESBITT

TOMMY DOWSON & BRIAN

TONY LEONARD

Tony weighed in at only 4lbs and was placed in an incubator for 2 weeks before being allowed home and had to be fed every 2 hours which Helen did during the day and evening. Keith Patterson the trio's drummer spent most of his time living with Brian & Helen. He got more than he bargained for when asked to help Brian on the night shift feeding baby Tony in-between playing cards and drinking Newcastle Brown Ale, a drop of which they were tempted to add to the bairn's bottle to get him to sleep! Although not wanting a career in entertainment Tony learned to play guitar and joined Davey Herron for private drum lessons and did on occasions play them at charity dos with his father. At age 16 Tony left school and joined the Junior Leaders Regiment, the name given to one of the training regiments of the British Army that took entrants from age 15 and through to adult service at the age of 17½. He had a very successful career in the Army although whilst undergoing training for special services a parachute accident left him with damaged feet and he transferred to the Royal Corps of Transport which didn't greatly appeal and he left at the age of 22. After a couple of jobs including roofing and long distance lorry driving Tony and his girlfriend Kath decided they would get married and he joined the British Transport Police at Kings Cross in London. After a few years he left the BTP and joined the Cambridgeshire Constabulary in Cambridge before eventually obtaining a posting to

North Yorkshire Police and Richmond where he is still stationed today. Tony & Kath have three children Ashley, Charley and Harry.

Turning Professional

Brian was still employed at Swan Hunters and was earning about £12 per week but really wanted to sing and play for a living and the trio were at that time coincidentally being paid £12 for a session in workingmen's clubs. So Brian proposed to Andy and Keith that they should consider turning professional. Andy Muat declined preferring to return to his career in the butchery business but Keith Patterson agreed and therefore Brian tendered his resignation at the shipyard.

As an organist & drummer duo, although both vocalists as well, they drove down to Nottingham with their equipment in a van and offered their services to a flourishing Club & Institute Union (CIU) scene and to where, following the closure of numerous North East mines in the late 50s and early 60s, many of its former miners had moved south for employment in the Nottinghamshire coalfields. *The Vance Clayton Duo*'s first engagement (a freebee as it happens) was at the Ollerton and Bevercotes Miners Welfare in the town of Ollerton in the Newark & Sherwood district of Nottinghamshire. When the duo arrived it had only been open a few years and had cost some £125,000 following the closure of the former club on the site opposite and, similar to the High Pit Club in Cramlington, had been dubbed the Palladium of the Midlands with big named stars appearing there. The American singer, songwriter and pianist Johnny Ray had been the opening act in November 1964. Like so many pubs and clubs across the country it closed its doors for the last time in 2009 and was subsequently demolished.

BRIAN & KEITH PATTERSON WHEN
THEY TURNED PROFESSIONAL

Paid engagements followed and Brian and Keith enjoyed some three weeks' work there before returning to the North East. With Andy having left the band to resume his butchery career Mick Nicholson was recruited to play guitar although he too eventually left after about 18 months. By the late 60s the *Vance Clayton Trio* was a big name on Tyneside and wowing audiences in all the top venues in the North East. One such location was the Bombers Club in Gateshead where the trio, Mick Nicholson on bass, Keith Patterson on drums and Brian on keyboards, worked most Sunday afternoons.

They congregated and played jam sessions with many other acts and groups which included a student band from Newcastle University called *Gas Board* with Graham Simpson, John Porter and Bryan Ferry. All three of that group would go on to excel in the music business, Bryan and Graham (who died in April 2012) with *Roxy Music* and John as a record producer. Also regulars there were a group called *The Influence* with Paul Thompson (later to become drummer with Roxy Music), Vic Malcolm (later lead guitarist with *Geordie*) and John Miles, vocalist, guitarist, keyboard player and songwriter who went on to form *The John Miles Set* before going solo in 1971 and having a UK No. 3 hit single entitled 'Music' in 1976.

Brian Leonard and John Miles would later become golfing friends with Ray Pearson the owner of Northern Floorcraft (Gateshead) Ltd and join the company's corporate golf days for some 7 years. They would play golf during the day and later do a cabaret spot featuring other top North East acts including Brendan Healey, the accomplished entertainer and musician. At one corporate event Brian went on to perform first followed by Brendan who said *"Let's hear it for Vance Clayton, we call him Spiderman not because he's a superhero just that he can't get out of the fucking bath!"*

One of Brian's biggest disappointments occurred around this time in his career when he along with Mick Nicholson and Keith Patterson were working in a night club in South Shields in early 1967 and were approached by Peter Shelley – a talent scout for Decca Records – who was very impressed by their rendition of *The Four Seasons'* 1964 hit 'Rag Doll' and its B-side 'Silence Is Golden'. He invited them, along with George Short a local drummer who had a good falsetto voice, to travel to a studio used by Decca in London to record demo tapes of 'Rag Doll', 'Walk Like A Man' and 'Silence Is Golden'. They did so and were told that their performance of 'Silence Is Golden' was excellent and could be used as a B-side on a record and that an appropriate A-side would be sought.

Some three months later in May 1967 Brian heard 'Silence Is Golden' being played on the radio only to find out that it wasn't his recording but that of *The Tremeloes*! The record sold over 1 million copies globally and earned *The Tremeloes* a gold disc. Peter Shelley (the talent scout) went on to perform as a solo artist in the 1970s having UK Top 10 hits with

'Gee Baby' (UK No. 4) and 'Love Me Love My Dog' (UK No. 3).

The Tremeloes had started out as *Brian Poole & The Tremeloes* in 1958 in Dagenham, East London and on New Year's Day 1962 were auditioned by Decca along with a Liverpool based group called *The Beatles*. Decca chose *Brian Poole & The Tremeloes* reportedly founded on the fact that they were London based and therefore more accessible. Brian Poole left the band in 1966 to pursue a solo career and the band's composition changed.

They downsized from a five piece to a quartet when the bassist Alan Howard also left in 1966 and was replaced by Chip Hawkes and three of the originals - Dave Munden on drums, Alan Blakley the keyboard player and Rick West as lead guitarist - completed the line up that had the hit with 'Silence Is Golden'. Chip Hawkes recalled in an interview that *The Tremeloes* had been touring with *The Hollies* in 1967 and receiving standing ovations for 'Silence Is Golden' and recorded it immediately and by the time the tour was over it was in the charts. Tony Hicks a guitarist with *The Hollies* (a Manchester based group) told him that it was a good job they did as they were going to cut it. Given Decca's obvious preference for London based groups at that point in time it is conceivable therefore that is why *The Tremeloes* got the nod over the *Vance Clayton Trio* and presumably other such hopefuls.

Although a huge disappointment at the time Brian now takes the view that had he had the huge success enjoyed by the likes of those bands he probably would not have survived and enjoyed the family life and career he has had.

Summer Seasons

Mick Nicholson subsequently left the trio and Dave Shipley, who had previously been in *The Gators* with Brian, left *The Delamares* the group he was with at the time and joined up with Brian again. In 1968 the *Vance Clayton Trio* with Brian, Keith Patterson & Dave Shipley were awarded the first of two Summer Season contracts at the Ocean Theatre on the pier in Clacton on Sea Essex.

During the Trio's first season in Clacton Helen Leonard gave birth to their second child, another beautiful son Paul, at home in Whickham on Wednesday the 31st July 1968. Brian rushed back on the Sunday night to see him, Helen & Tony and a couple of weeks later they all joined Brian in Essex for the rest of the season. They stayed in a tiny one roomed wooden shack in Jaywick Sands Holiday village near Clacton. With only room for a double bed and a cot for Tony, baby Paul was put in the bottom drawer of a chest of drawers. Even though times were tough and the money they earned was a pittance they all survived!

MICK NICHOLSON – BRIAN – KEITH PATTERSON

BRIAN – DAVE SHIPLEY – KEITH PATTERSON
CLACTON

BILLING POSTER
OCEAN THEATRE CLACTON ON SEA

PAUL LEONARD

At the tender age of nine months baby Paul contracted meningitis and that sadly resulted in him developing epilepsy which often occurs in such cases following the damage to the nervous system that inflammation of the brain's membrane causes. Nevertheless he has coped very well with the disability, went to agricultural college and had a career as a gardener with Gateshead Council, married and raised a family. Paul received brain surgery in 2002 which alleviated the increasing severity of his disability for a few years but some five years ago his condition deteriorated and necessitated him leaving his paid employment. He has the support of a loving family; including his children Tim and Kathryn who have learned to help Lisa, their mother, cope very well with Paul's condition.

Also appearing at the Ocean Theatre Clacton was a magician called Harold Taylor (1913-1993) whose stage career had started in The Windmill Theatre in London after the Second World War and led to him performing many cabaret shows for the rich and famous. These including performing for the young Royals in Buckingham Palace, Windsor Castle and Sandringham, three parties at No 10 Downing Street and seventeen Christmas shows for Jean Paul Getty. He also had a magic slot on the children's TV show called Crackerjack in the 1960s. Brian remembers that Harold had a show called the *Harold Taylor Party* show in which he had a large box on stage filled with toys, hats and balloons for the kids and would invite them on stage singing *"Dip into the magic box, the magic box"* which also contained tins of HP Baked Beans and he would manipulate what they got in their hands! Brian would ask Harold to make sure that when any of the trio's children dipped they got baked beans which would help supplement their weekly provisions. Brian will never forget the kids' reactions when his Tony would exclaim *"Oh no not another tin of beans – I get beans every week!"* and Dave Shipley's bairn would cry *"I got beans as well!"*

Whilst working there Brian made friends with a couple from Sunderland who were living in Clacton at that time. Nan worked on the pier selling tickets and her husband Tom would come to see the shows and became a great fan of the trio. Brian was invited back to their bungalow in the centre of Clacton where Tom grew his own vegetables and knowing that the trio were only making just enough to get by and Helen was feeding everyone he would give Brian loads of produce to take back to their accommodation. In return Brian would play the piano for him and help Tom practice and they became very good friends and for many years would exchange Christmas cards until with house moves etc., they sadly lost touch with each other. However in the summer of 2013 when Brian & Davey Herron were performing at the Wearside golf club near Sunderland a very attractive lady approached Brian in the bar during the interval and asked if he was *Vance Clayton* and had he performed at the pier in Clacton back in the late 60s. She explained that she was the granddaughter of Tom & Nan and remembered Brian going to their home to help her granddad with his piano lessons. She further explained that her mother had died prematurely and her grandparents had moved back to Sunderland to look after her. Both Tom & Nan had lived until they were 94 years old.

The owner of the Jaywick Sands Holiday Park, a man called Tony Jolley, approached Brian and asked if the trio would like to play at his club on a Sunday night – it being their night off from the pier – and although he couldn't afford to pay them he would give them as much beer as they could drink! He clearly hadn't heard about the reputation Geordies have for drink. The lads would drink Double Diamond all night and then carry quantities back to their accommodation in large plastic containers and drink until the early hours. By the end of the second Sunday night the owner told them that he had never known men to drink quite so much and had decided to pay them fifteen quid (£15) instead of free drink. The trio had a Ford Transit van to transport their equipment around in and which was parked up for most of the season as they couldn't afford to run it. However they had a 'Del Boy' three-wheeler car which did about 70 miles to the gallon and they used to ferry themselves from their accommodation to the Clacton venue and a gallon of petrol would last them almost a week. It would however routinely run out on a Thursday night about half a mile from the venue and they would have to walk in, borrow the 6s 3d (around 30p) to fill a gallon can and refill the car and get back to their accommodation.

Matt Monro

Having finished their first Summer Season the Trio were booked to support Matt Monro, for a week in the Fiesta Club in Stockton on Tees. Matt Monro was one of the most popular entertainers on the international music scene in the 60s with hit singles including 'Portrait Of My Love' (UK No.3), 'My Kind Of Girl' (UK No. 5), 'Softly As I Leave You' (UK No.10), 'Walk Away' (UK No. 4) and 'Yesterday' (UK No. 8). Their initial meeting at the club didn't get off to the best of starts occasioned by the trio unknowingly parking their Ford Transit van in Matt's allocated parking space. He appeared at the door of their dressing room in his string vest wanting to know *"Whose bloody Transit's that parked in my space?"* *"That'll be mine"* Brian replied. *"Never mind 'mine' here's my keys – get it shifted"* and walked out. *"Big headed bugger"* muttered Brian but Dave Shipley pulled the Transit van out and shifted Matt's Rolls Royce (registration number MM 1) into the space even though there was plenty of room elsewhere in the car park. A short time later Matt reappeared and thanked them for shifting the van and parking his Roller and informed them that they were to use his dressing room for the rest of the week and they would have a few drinks together and enjoy the week.

According to Brian he turned out to be one of the nicest artists he ever worked with and the best singer he ever heard. Brian greatly admired his voice control and although not wishing to make a comparison acknowledged that Matt Monro would take only one breath to sing a phrase whereas it would take him three. A couple of days into the week Matt was pulled off the stage by over enthusiastic ladies in the audience and cracked his ribs. He was taken to hospital where they strapped him up and, trouper that he was, he still fulfilled the rest of the engagement. They were to meet again when the trio were working in Africa and Matt Monro appeared there too.

Guy Mitchell

During their second season in Clacton in 1969 the trio met up with an entertainer called Eddie Buchanan who mixed stand-up comedy with a great voice. Although Manchester born Eddie learned his trade on the North East club circuit and suggested to Brian and the other two lads that they join up as a four piece - *Eddie Buchanan and The Vance Clayton Trio*. So they did a few rehearsals and produced a fantastic show and eventually toured all over the North of England playing upmarket nightclubs in Manchester, Liverpool etc. As time went on however Eddie started to take over, doing his impressions and comedy routine and leaving the trio just playing the Batchelors and Platters hits - maybe all night. It therefore got to the point after some 4 months or so where the lads weren't doing any real work, forgetting all their songs and the music they had learned over time and so they decided to put an end to it. Eddie Buchanan went on to become a regular guest artiste on the Benny Hill TV Show playing various roles and performing musical numbers along with Henry McGee and Don Estelle. Sadly Eddie lost his long battle with heart disease and died in the Royal Victoria Infirmary Newcastle in April 1987 aged 47.

Beverley Artistes were the trio's agents at this point in time and Brian took a call from them requesting 'a big favour' which raised immediate concerns in his mind. *"We've booked GUY MITCHELL from the States"* stated the agent. *"What THE Guy Mitchell?"* inquired Brian *"He's bloody brilliant and sold more records than Frank Sinatra"* he enthused. The agent went on to explain that he had already done two gigs for them and that they'd nearly paid him off because the band he'd got backing him were just kids, hadn't got any music and didn't know his repertoire. Brian asked whether the agent wanted the trio to back him. *"If you wouldn't mind?"* came the agent's response, *"and take him round the venues and look after him"*. *"Mind he's an alcoholic so you'll need to keep him off the drink before he goes on stage"* the agent warned.

They all met up and introduced themselves and Beverley Artistes bought a Guy Mitchell album and gave it to Brian for him and the lads to listen to and follow his repertoire, although they knew most of his stuff anyway including 'My Truly, Truly Fair' (US No. 2), 'She Wears Red Feathers' (UK No. 1), 'Pretty Little Black Eyed Susie' (UK No. 2) and 'Singing The Blues' (US & UK No. 1). The tour, which lasted four weeks, entailed playing one working men's club at 8 o'clock and two nightclubs per night, one at 10 o'clock and the other at midnight and as they drove between venues Guy would cry out *"There's a bar – stop and we'll get a brandy"* as they passed almost every 'watering hole' in the North East. The request would be ritually refused such that he at least *arrived* at the venue sober.

Brian would introduce him on stage as follows *"Ladies and Gentlemen all the way from America, the super star Mr Guy Mitchell"* and Guy would open up with *"You're my truly, truly fair – truly, truly fair......"* and promptly put down the microphone and walk into the audience, shaking hands whilst Brian sang *".....how I love my truly fair"* and completed the song. This happened with most of his numbers as he would sing a verse and a chorus and then disappear into the crowd shaking hands and knocking back their drinks. By the time he came off stage he was very nearly *plastered*.

One night they were appearing at the Bird Cage nightclub (later to be renamed the Stage Door) in Stowell Street Newcastle. With its casino it was a favourite haunt of lovers of nightlife - both locals and visitors to the city. On the night in question Dorothy Squires the singer, although separated was still legally married to Roger Moore, approached Brian and asked if she could go on stage and sing with Guy Mitchell. Brian told her it was no problem and asked what she was going to sing – 'Me and My Shadow' came the answer. Guy & Dorothy brought the house down as they shimmied around the stage singing 'Me and My Shadow'. Dorothy Squires was Welsh born and one of the most popular singing stars of the 1940s, 50s, 60s and 70s on both sides of the Atlantic with hits such as 'I'm Walking Behind You', 'Say It With Flowers', 'For Once In My Life', 'Till' and 'My Way' and her last live show was in the Brighton Dome in March 1990 almost 54 years after she made her recording debut. A young Elvis Presley was one of her biggest fans in the USA and would ask her to sing 'This Is My Mother's Day'. Diagnosed with cancer in 1996 she died at home in Mid-Glamorgan in April 1998.

The night after the Bird Cage club incident the trio and Guy were booked at the Playboy Club in Seaham Co. Durham where *Tony Christie and The Pen Men* were also playing. At that stage they were just a journeyman club act and it wasn't until the early seventies, and after Christie had gone solo in 1969, that he achieved Top 10 hits with 'I Did What I Did For Maria' and 'Is This The Way To Amarillo'. Guy Mitchell had been told about the group and mentioned during his performance that there was an up and coming band in the audience. Tony Christie went to see Brian and told him that he didn't want to sing with the *Vance Clayton Trio* backing him as he had his own band and they would play for him. Although Brian had told him they were only to do one number they did about 20 minutes by which time Guy had consumed a fair amount of alcohol and eventually had a job to finish his performance. Brian remonstrated with Christie after the show, telling him that it was less than professional to try and upstage an artist who had sold more records than he, Tony Christie, could possibly dream of and told him how Guy had duetted with Dorothy Squires the night before and brought the house down.

Over the month as they toured together, Brian and the lads grew to enjoy Guy's company and they ended up the best of pals even though the lads had to nurse him along the way before he returned to America. Including repeatedly repairing his spectacles which Guy would leave lying around the place to be sat or stood upon. Their paths were to cross again later in their respective travels.

On the road

There were of course dozens of bands playing the pubs and clubs in those days, including *Al Meechie & The Pyramids, The Bodysnatchers and Freddie Starr & The Delmonts* and they would regularly pass each other on the road and between venues and recognise each other's transport usually Transit vans. Mooning, or the art of displaying one's bare buttocks by removing clothing and bending over, was known of in the 17th century and the practice widespread by the 19th century and it became popular again in the 1960s. It was used by band members as a form of acknowledgement or greeting as they passed each other or people that they knew. At that time the legal position related to mooning varied depending on how well the 'offender' or 'offenders' were known by the police and certainly today it is classed as indecent exposure.

In that regard Jimmy Allan (Brian's old school pal) had a close encounter all those years ago when he had finished an early evening cabaret performance with *This, That and The Other* at Bobby Pattinson's club The Talk Of The Tyne in Gateshead. He had dropped the other two members off and had driven his van to Saltwell Social Club where he called in for a drink before making his way home. He had a few more drinks than he should have had and on returning to his van found out the exhaust pipe was hanging off. He got a guitar string from the back of the van and got under the vehicle to temporarily secure the exhaust and whilst doing so observed four black shiny shoes appear beside him. *"'Ello 'Ello what's going on under there?"* came the enquiry! *"Oh shit the police!"* exclaimed Jimmy as he pulled himself from under the van but immediately recognised the two coppers and they in turn acknowledged him. *"Oh it's you Jimmy"* said one of the policemen *"What you doing under there?"* Jimmy explained that he had been playing the early spot at Pattinson's club in Gateshead and called in at Saltwell club for a drink before going home and found out that the exhaust had come loose and was making emergency repairs. *"Had much to drink Jimmy?"* enquired one of the Bobbies, *"Quite a few"* replied Jimmy. *"Well, take it easy and get yourself home safely"* was the advice!

Jimmy finished what he was doing and pulled out of the club car park, drove to the top of the road and turned left and saw a police car parked on the opposite side of the road. He immediately stopped the van, wound down the window, dropped his pants and showed the occupants his backside only to realise that it wasn't the two he'd been talking to and they were complete strangers to him. With a couple of minutes head start a hectic chase all over Gateshead ensued but Jimmy got back home to Dunston unscathed!

During their travels and work experiences the lads in the *Vance Clayton Trio* would witness other artists performing around the club circuits and in due course saw a jazz-oriented group called *The Peddlers,* singing songs such as 'Smile (Though Your Heart Is Aching)' composed by Charlie Chaplin and charted by Nat King Cole - but with a jazz feel which the lads and lots of other performers thought was great. Brian and the other two lads decided to include some of *The Peddlers* numbers in their own shows and use their style. It didn't go down well with their audiences but as Brian recollects *"we were young and stupid and thought we knew best"*. Their agent at the time thought differently and told Brian in no uncertain terms that they also booked *The Peddlers* and couldn't get *them* 'bloody work' so they were to cut it out because people in the clubs didn't want to listen to it. He instructed the band to either revert to singing the material they were doing before like *The Batchelors* and *The Platters* hits or he wouldn't be able to book them again. He further told them he had booked them at La Ronde, a nightclub in Billingham on Teesside for a week as the resident band and that this was their last chance.

Also appearing on the bill one night that week at La Ronde was a group called *Mud* with Les Gray lead vocalist, Rob Davis lead guitarist, Ray Stiles bass guitarist and the drummer Dave Mount who were still relatively unknown outside the club circuits and hadn't yet hit the big time with 'Tiger Feet' and 'Lonely This Christmas'. Towards the end of their cabaret spot Mud started to perform a medley of sing-a-long songs such as 'Heart Of My Heart', 'What D'ya Wanna (Make Those Eyes At Me For)' and 'Slow Boat To China' and the whole audience joined in. Brian and the lads looked at each other and thought *'what the hell have we been doing these last few months, singing all that crap by The Peddlers?'* and instantly decided to go back to their old style of playing.

TONY & KATHLEEN LEONARD'S WEDDING

ASHLEY & NIGEL HERON'S WEDDING

LISA & PAUL LEONARD'S WEDDING

ANNABEL & BILLY
LEONARD'S WEDDING

ELDEST SON TONY

MIDDLE SON PAUL   YOUNGEST SON BILLY

TONY & KATHLEEN'S
ELDEST DAUGHTER
ASHLEY

TONY & KATHLEEN'S
SON HARRY

TONY & KATHLEEN'S
YOUNGEST DAUGHTER
CHARLEY

PAUL & LISA'S SON TIM

PAUL & LISA'S
DAUGHTER KATHRYN

BILLY & ANNABEL'S
SON CURTIS

BILLY & ANNABEL'S
DAUGHTER KELLY

HELEN & BRIAN

BRIAN LEWIS – HELEN – BRIAN THIS IS
YOUR LIFE 40 YRS IN BUSINESS

BRIAN – TONY – HARRY THREE GENERATIONS
ON STAGE AT ASHLEY'S WEDDING

DAVE SHIPLEY – FRANK CARSON
– JOHN SIDDLE – BRIAN, BUTLINS

JOHN SIDDLE – BRIAN – LES DENNIS
– DAVE SHIPLEY, BUTLINS

IAN WRIGHT – BRIAN – DAVE SHIPLEY – LARRY MASON
– KIM – MANAGER – ALAN FOX – CHEF AT ALAN'S 60TH
BIRTHDAY AT DIXIELANDERS SUNDERLAND

DAVE SHIPLEY – IAN WRIGHT – ALAN SNELL
– REBECCA STORM – ALAN FOX – BRIAN

BRIAN – ALAN ROBERTS, BUTLINS

BRIAN – DAVEY HERRON – STEVE (DONKEY MAN)
– JIM MEADOWCROFT – ROGER WOODCOCK – BARRY REDMAN

ALAN ROBERTS – SHEILA
– BRIAN – IAN WRIGHT

DRUMMER FROM SPANISH BAR BAND (DAVE SMITH SET) & BRIAN

IAN WRIGHT – BRIAN
– DAVE SHIPLEY – MALLY (REDCOAT)

IAN WRIGHT – BRIAN – ALAN FOX – CINDY KELLY – HUGHIE
TURNER – DIANE TURNER – DAVE SHIPLEY – DIANE'S
BOYFRIEND AT FEDERATION BREWERY, DUNSTON

DAVEY HERRON – BRIAN – BARRY REDMAN AT BUTLINS

Rhodesia

Just a couple of weeks later a man called Miles Knox from Teesside who was also a music agent in Rhodesia (an unrecognised state in Southern Africa from 1965 to 1979 and formerly called Southern Rhodesia) now known as Zimbabwe, saw the trio playing in Stockton and told them he'd love them to go to Rhodesia. Brian thought *where the hell is Rhodesia?* as he'd never heard of it. To cut a long story short the three lads eventually decided to sign up with Miles. Of course that meant that Brian had to break the news to Helen, who with Brian and their two young children had only recently moved into their new home in Whickham. Not unnaturally Helen wanted to know how long her husband would be away. Three months, Brian informed her and with some trepidation she agreed.

Having made a Unilateral Declaration of Independence from the British Crown on 11th November 1965, Ian Smith the Rhodesian Prime Minister embarked on leading a minority white and illegal government. The UK government lead by Harold Wilson responded by immediately announcing a full range of sanctions rather than a British military intervention which both Rhodesian opposition parties had called for. Later in the year the United Nations Security Council unanimously passed Resolution 217 adding member states' sanctions against Smith's illegal regime. Nonetheless white minority rule continued in Rhodesia until 1st June

1979 when it gained independence from Great Britain as Zimbabwe on 18th April 1980 with Robert Mugabe as its head of state.

Sanctions against Rhodesia were therefore still in force when Brian, Keith Patterson & Dave Shipley made the decision to venture out there in 1970. Those sanctions included the export of any item to Rhodesia (except for humanitarian purposes) and airlines were prohibited from operating flights to or from the country. Two of Rhodesia's neighbours however, South Africa and the Portuguese colonial regime in Mozambique, openly rejected sanctions including the flights embargo.

Miles Knox, the agent, arranged all the flights which as a result of sanctions meant no direct flight to Rhodesia and therefore required a journey via South Africa. Brian had only ever been on a short flight once before, had hated the experience and faced with such a lengthy flight to Johannesburg in South Africa before the connection to Salisbury in Rhodesia he did what many had done before, and still try - he got mortal drunk. The trio flew out to Africa in May 1970 and he remembers the stewardess announcing the landing at Jo'burg saying *"Welcome to Jan Smuts Airport Johannesburg ladies and gentlemen - please turn your watches back twenty years"*. She wasn't far wrong as Brian recalls. South Africa's white minority government, under the National Party's apartheid regime, were struggling with the cost of the new technologies and in 1970 it is estimated there were only about 400 computers in the country with a value of around US$100m. The South African government viewed television, for instance, as a potential threat to its control of the broadcasting media, even though the state-controlled South African Broadcasting Corporation had a virtual monopoly on radio broadcasting. It also saw the new medium as a threat to the Afrikaans language and to Afrikaners, giving undue prominence to English, and creating unfair competition for the Afrikaans press. TV was therefore not introduced into South Africa until 1976 unlike Rhodesia where it had started in 1960.

When Brian, Keith Patterson & Dave Shipley finally arrived in Rhodesia they found out that although it was indeed a three months contract they had signed up for, there was a nine months option to extend but on the agency's side NOT theirs! Their agent, Miles Knox, had booked them into a hotel in Salisbury (not the finest it has to be said) for the first 2 or 3 days because unfortunately, and due to the sanctions, their musical equipment was detained at Heathrow Airport in London.

Miles then rented them a luxury 4 bedroom bungalow complete with swimming pool, tennis court etc. They shared this with Miles and his girlfriend, the singer Kerry James, and it had a couple of servants – a garden boy and a housekeeper who did all the catering, cleaning etc. Their contract, six nights a week with Sundays off, entailed working a fashionable nightclub in Salisbury called Bretts and every Saturday night at 8pm they were the resident group in a live one hour show called Night Club Scene in a small local TV station. Brian was also part of the jury on the TV station's version of Juke Box Jury every Thursday night and he would take along whoever was appearing at Bretts that week to form a show business knowledgeable jury. Miles Knox and Billy Fontaine, who was the resident compere and comedian at Bretts, would occasionally join the panel. Brian's fee was a princely R$8 (c£4) a night.

The trio's first engagement was a dinner cabaret show in Bretts but shortly after their arrival Brian got bitten by a spider and just before appearing his leg swelled up to about twice its normal size and he actually passed out on stage. After half an hour in the fresh air he recovered enough to carry on but later passed out again and was hospitalised and given injections and medication.

Their ongoing work at Bretts also involved the trio supporting and backing the club's solo entertainers including a relaxed and easy on the ear baritone with shades of Val Doonican and Bing Crosby called Glenn Irving from England who had appeared with and supported many top show business names in and around the UK. Glenn eventually emigrated from UK to Rhodesia in 1972 where he enjoyed great success both in cabaret and on TV in Rhodesia, South and South West Africa until 1975 when family problems back in the UK forced his return there. He is now a successful wildlife artist specialising in African elephant and lion studies in oil, pastel and ink.

The first three months flew by and the *Vance Clayton Trio* proved to be an enormous success and as a consequence the nine month option on their contract was duly taken up. After about six months Helen called time on the 'separation' and along with the other trio 'widows' similarly decided to join their menfolk in Rhodesia. Helen therefore gave up the house in Whickham and with their two boys, Tony and Paul she flew out on 2nd January 1971 along with Dave Shipley's wife Heather and their two daughters Melanie and Joanne and son Nicholas and Keith Patterson's wife Mary and son Mark.

It proved to be a somewhat difficult and harrowing trip for Helen. The flight schedules meant she had to break the journey in Nairobi Kenya for a couple of days. She was initially refused entry at Jomo Kenyatta airport for the reason that she was wearing a miniskirt and because their entire luggage was booked through to Salisbury she had to borrow something to cover her legs.

Dave Shipley and his wife Heather and the three children moved into the Kamfinsa Hotel in Salisbury which was run by a couple from Sunderland called Harry and Fran Clifton who also ran the Geordie Club of Rhodesia. Brian, Helen and the two boys Tony & Paul along with Keith Patterson, his wife Mary and son Mark took over the bungalow the trio had previously occupied. This situation lasted for about 3 or 4 months until they all ended up living in the Kamfinsa Hotel until the end of the contract.

Bretts regularly featured international entertainers including Dickie Valentine, Eve Boswell, Lita Roza, *Karl Denver Trio*, Wayne Fontana and Billy J Kramer. Both Wayne Fontana and Billy J Kramer were there as solo performers and were backed by the *Vance Clayton Trio*. Wayne Fontana, born Glyn Geoffrey Ellis, loved to play cards and would join the trio after performances sometimes playing until two or three o'clock in the morning.

Karl Denver, born Angus Murdo Mackenzie, made several visits to Rhodesia and he and Brian formed a good friendship. Apparently Angus' youngest son, called Karl, had tragically died in an accident and having lived for a while in Denver Colorado USA he decided to assume Karl Denver as his stage name. He did a lot of charity work and when in Rhodesia helped out at a lot of events for the nuns who ran the local orphanage. On one occasion the Mother Superior came to pick Karl up and took him to the orphanage where he put on a great show for the kids. However the Mother Superior subsequently put in a complaint to the management at Bretts reporting that on the way into the orphanage she had tripped on some steps and Karl had said in his thick Yorkshire accent *"Eh up ya silly ole cow pissed again!"* She didn't drink!

Brian also recalls one pleasant Sunday afternoon

(their day off) they were all sitting around drinking, Karl with a whisky and a packet of Capstan Full Strength cigarettes close at hand when they were approached by a local dental technician, who had an unfortunate stutter, and asked if they would all like to go out to his place that evening where he was holding a party. He explained that Ian Smith, the Prime Minister and the Lord Mayor of Salisbury along with other dignitaries had been invited. Karl, Brian and the rest of the lads agreed they would attend later that evening. Karl said to Brian *"That bugger wants us to do a show for nought that's why we're invited!"* By the time they arrived at the party Smith had left but the Lord Mayor and many others were still in attendance. Sure enough and as Karl had predicted the host sidled up and stuttered *"K- KKarl w-wwould you d- ddo a s -sshow for us?"* *"Oh sure"* replied Karl, *"We'll get the guitars from the car"* and instructed the host to give them five minutes to prepare and to close the curtains on the patio doors such that the trio could go out into the garden behind the curtains and carry out their performance. The host then announced *"Ll- ladies and Gg -gents all the w- wway from England the K -kkarl D- ddenver Trio"* and opened the curtains. To everyone's amazement there were the trio stood 'stark bollock-naked' with just their Stetsons on singing 'Wimoweh'. The curtains shut as fast as an express train with the host having lost his stutter shouting *"No, no you can't do that!!!"* but everyone had fallen about laughing.

Karl used to perform magic tricks one of which

involved the silver foil from a cigarette packet and a powder he carried in a little pouch. In a similar mischievous vein to the dentist's party piece Karl went to see a witch doctor in his hut and told him that he had heard he was a good witch doctor. Karl then told him that he was white witch doctor and asked if he had any cigarettes. The witch doctor produced a packet of cigarettes and Karl removed some of the silver foil, dipped it in water and rubbed some of the powder onto the foil and screwed it into a ball and placed it on the open palm of the witch doctor's hand. It instantly turned hot and the witch doctor ran screaming from the hut with Karl in hot pursuit shouting *"I'm a better witch doctor than you!!!"* Indigenous Rhodesians gave him the nickname 'Boaty Maseteno' which is *Matabele* for 'brother of Satan'.

There was another night club in Salisbury called La Boheme and they were in direct competition with Bretts and the compere Ray Curtis, coincidentally a Geordie, would regularly taunt the trio with quips like *'I was in Bretts last night and a waiter dropped a tray and everyone got up to dance - the band was that bad!'.* One day he came into the club and said *"Clayton we're going to knack you this next fortnight – we've got Guy Mitchell coming out!"* Sure enough Guy Mitchell arrived at La Boheme minus his spectacles which he'd smashed again. The club had a resident Portuguese band who'd never heard of Guy Mitchell let alone played his music and were totally unprepared to back him. As a consequence Ray the compere rushed around to Bretts, cap in hand, apologising to Brian and explaining that they'd spent a lot of money getting Guy out only to find that their band couldn't back him and could Brian help. Brian told the compere that he knew Guy very well and would try to help out knowing, as Brian put it, that the band at La Boheme read music like tonic sol-fa (i.e. do, re, mi, fa, sol, la, ti, do). So the trio went along to the club in the afternoon and found Guy, not unusually, as 'high as a kite'. Without his glasses he didn't recognise Brian, Dave and Keith. Guy asked if he was going to show the band how to play his music to which Brian replied that he was and Brian, Keith, Dave and Ray proceeded to the stage where the club's band were already waiting. Brian sat down at the piano and told Ray the compere how to introduce Guy – *Guy Mitchell all the way from America* – and that he opened up with 'Truly Fair', at which point Brian, Keith & Dave started to play with Brian singing *Truly, truly fair, truly, truly fair How I love my truly fair* ... and showing the organist how to go on when he heard Guy call out *"Brian is that you and Dave and Keith? Not Brian from Newcastle - it can't be you?"* He went up to Brian and told him he had busted his glasses again and asked if he was going to back him like he had when he toured in the North East. Brian explained that he wasn't as they were in competition at another club and that Guy had to stay at La Boheme. Brian taught the organist the Guy Mitchell repertoire and Dave and Keith in turn taught the guitarist and drummer and the Portuguese band backed him quite successfully for the fortnight.

The TV show Night Club Scene was a great success and featured many of the top artistes who appeared at Bretts nightclub along with the *Vance Clayton Trio* and Kerry James. There being no video in those days Night Club Scene was recorded on reel to reel tapes which Brian would review with the Director of the show on a Tuesday or Wednesday of the following week and select and cut pieces which were saved for compiling into an end of the year charity event in Salisbury at Christmas 1971 called the Mayor's Christmas Cheer. It was a three hour show and took a similar form to the present day BBC TV show Children in Need hosted each year by Terry Wogan. Viewers would pledge money in return for Brian and the lads playing a request or be shown taped performances of the featured artistes who had appeared at Bretts including Dickie Valentine, Lita Roza, *Karl Denver Trio*, Billy J Kramer, Wayne Fontana and a host of other artistes. Brian also recalls having to bare his backside for a R$50 pledge!

An introduction to the Christmas show was required and having watched episodes of the American TV series Mission: Impossible in which the leader of the IMF (Impossible Missions Force) would get the assignment from a hidden tape recorder and an envelope of photos and information that explained their mission, Brian came up with the idea of a modification for the Christmas show. It involved photographs of all the artistes who had appeared on the weekly Night Club Scene TV show throughout the year being thrown down one at a time onto a pile and the last one being the *Vance Clayton Trio* who then appeared live in the studio opening the show with a medley of Christmas songs. It proved to be a great success.

GLENN IRVING - HARRY & FRAN CLIFTON - THE VANCE CLAYTON TRIO - MILES KNOX & KERRY JAMES AT THE KAMFINSA HOTEL

ON THE TV SET OF THE MAYOR'S CHRISTMAS CHEER SHOW

Miles Knox also booked other entertainment in Rhodesia and amongst other things promoted professional wrestling and brought out 'Big' Pat Roach from Birmingham England for a series of matches. By this time Miles and his girlfriend had found alternative accommodation and Pat was billeted with Brian and the lads in the spare room of the bungalow. When they first met up Brian told Pat that he, like many others, thought professional wrestling was a 'load of bull' and a big con! Well Pat was as 'hard as nails' and promptly gripped Brian by the left and right shoulders and in pressurising nerves immediately paralysed both sides of his body leaving him a crumpled heap on the floor. Pat explained to Brian that that was some of the treatment he regularly received in the ring as opponents found appropriate nerves in the body. They subsequently established a great relationship for the remainder of Pat's stay in Salisbury and enjoyed each other's company over a few drinks in the club.

One night Brian, Keith and Dave were suited up
and getting ready to leave for their cabaret work in
Bretts and Pat had dressed ready to join them for a
night out and asked Brian to get his camera in order
to take a photo of him with Dave Shipley. Well Dave
couldn't swim and hated the water and Pat must
have gotten to know this and picked him up with
one hand and held him out like a rag doll repeatedly
asking Brian if he could get them both in the frame
as he deliberately backed up towards the edge of
the swimming pool. As he reached the pool he fell
back still holding on to Dave and both ended up like
drowned rats. Needless to say Dave played the bass
that night wearing a different style suit to that of
Brian & Keith.

Brian has fond memories of Pat Roach, that larger
than life, very popular man who apparently felt no
pain and would, as party tricks, push safety pins
through his nose and hands. Pat Roach went on to
become an actor and appeared as the West Country
bricklayer, Brian 'Bomber' Busbridge in the hit UK
TV comedy-drama series Auf Wiedersehen Pet with
Jimmy Nail, Tim Healy, Kevin Whateley and Timothy
Spall. He was the only actor apart from Harrison
Ford to appear in all three films in the Indiana Jones
trilogy. He died in 2004 aged 67 after a long fight
with throat cancer.

Towards the end of their contract Miles Knox their
agent, who had been getting acts in and out of
Rhodesia from the UK, had run up considerable

financial credit with the airline and was consequently in debt for some R$3,000 and couldn't raise the cash. As a result he was jailed because it was thought he would 'do a runner' and leave the country. Miles asked Brian if he could help and undertook to reimburse him when they got back to UK. Brian agreed and sold his organ for R$3,000 paid off the debt and got Miles out of jail. However Miles subsequently got the money from the UK and paid Brian back who was then left without an organ and had to play piano until they got an old Hammond organ from a church and the Bretts contract was over. Brian and Miles still keep in touch and Miles claims to be forever in Brian's debt having 'saved his bacon'. He was a bit of a hard man as was exemplified one night at the club when a world ranked boxer came in and caused some bother and started pushing people around. Miles threw him out and in so doing head butted him really hard and blackened his eye such that apparently he had to call off his next fight. *"They're not the Queensbury rules!"* the boxer shouted during the mêlée – *"No these are Seaham Harbour rules!"* retorted Miles.

Bretts was part-owned by Ian Sandeman of Sandeman's Port and shortly before the trio's contract ended it was sold to a South African called A A (Uppy) Olivier and owner of the discotheque The Tomorrow in Johannesburg. He employed a Portuguese exotic dancer named Amber, a really bonny lass with long black hair, for the three weeks before the lads left. At this point in time Miles Knox arranged a tour of Rhodesia for the trio in a show along with Billy Fontaine, as compere and comedian, a stripper called Axa and a brilliant Mario Lanza type tenor named Julian Jorg who probably weighed about 22 stones. The 3 week tour was sponsored by Coca Cola and Rothmans cigarettes – Coca Cola providing an old gangster-style Chevrolet car with running boards and Rothmans supplying batches of King Size cigarettes for them to give away. They loaded the car with Davey's bass guitar, Keith's drum kit and a PA system together with their clothes and the six of them set off for Bulawayo to their first concert venue. Having already sold his organ to save Miles's neck Brian had to use whatever piano was available at the concert venues some of which wouldn't have passed bonfire night according to Brian. Bulawayo however was a great venue, similar in size to Newcastle's City Hall and had a baby grand piano which suited Brian down to the ground. It was packed out and the show went off extremely well.

The following day they travelled to Kariba Dam in the Kariba Gorge of the Zambezi river basin between Zambia and Rhodesia where the show took place in a church hall and Brian had to play an out-of-tune piano acquired from someone's house. However it was a good night and everyone enjoyed themselves. The tour continued in some six or seven other venues around Rhodesia including Victoria Falls where they performed to a large audience in a big hotel. Then it was back to Salisbury to say farewell to everyone in Bretts night club after two years.

South Africa

Afterwards the trio, along with Kerry James, flew out of Rhodesia to Durban in South Africa for a two week appearance at the Mayfair Supper Club – a select uptown night club. Helen, along with Dave Shipley's wife Heather and their daughters Melanie & Joanne and son Nicholas, Keith Patterson's wife Mary and their son Mark, had promised the kids they would show them African wildlife including lions etc. Rather than fly they embarked on a three day luxury sleeper journey by rail from Rhodesia to South Africa via Botswana but all they saw were wildebeest. Consequently they had to take the kids to the zoo to see the lions after they arrived in Durban!

Then it was on to Port Elizabeth for a week's engagement for Brian, the lads and Kerry James while Helen and the two boys stayed in Durban in a hotel owned by Miles Knox called the Wagon Wheels. After Port Elizabeth it was on to East London and a 5 star hotel called the King's Hotel which had a small basement night club where the trio were pleased to meet up and appear with Matt Monro again. Helen and the bairns joined Brian there and they lived in a rented house just up the hill from the hotel although taking advantage of all the luxury hotel had to offer including food. Part of Brian's duties was to play background music on the grand piano in the hotel's foyer between 5 and 6pm and he would embarrass Helen when she walked in with the kids for their tea by launching into the Laurel and Hardy theme tune –

'Dance Of The Cuckoos'!

Helen made friends with the local coloured, black and Asian people including the servant girl who came with the rented accommodation and would sit and talk with them. She would also take over the laundry by doing the washing and ironing which were strictly part of the black girl's duties. Although fabulous food was available at the hotel Helen would often round up a bunch of local coloured and Asian kids and along with her two boys take them to the 'whites only' beach for a picnic. She even went to a local store and bought a primus stove and pan and would cook them hot dogs and beans. The children loved it but because of the apartheid laws which segregated people into four racial groups – indigenous, white, coloured and Asian – local white people objected while Helen rightly claimed *"bairns are bairns whatever their colour!"*. This proved a turning point for her and already missing her Mam and with the kids needing schooling and disapproving of the white people's attitude towards the other racial groups she decided to leave South Africa and returned home to live with her mother.

The trio carried on for another six months until one night a lad in his late 20s came into the night club drunk, acting himself and fell over Keith's drums damaging one of the drum skins so Keith took hold of him, bundled him outside and taught him a lesson. However it transpired that the lad was a multi-millionaire, who regularly frequented the hotel, spent a lot of money there and did business with them. Consequently the owner of the hotel called Brian in and advised him that although the young man was out of order Keith had blacked his eye and bloodied his nose and felt that Keith should apologise otherwise he would have to terminate their contract. Brian explained the situation to Keith and said it was up to him whether or not he was prepared to oblige. The next day a meeting was arranged with the owner, the young man concerned, Keith, Dave and Brian at which the owner formally introduced the man to Keith. Keith said *"Yes I remember him – he came in the club 'pissed as a fart', fell over my drums and made a complete arsehole of himself"*. The owner explained that all would be forgotten if Keith apologised. Keith told him that he had about as much chance of getting an apology as a flight to the moon and if he ever came near him again he would knack him again. With that the trio turned around and walked out of the office only for Brian to be called back in and offered the opportunity to work for the owner touring South Africa looking for cabaret acts. Brian politely declined the offer informing the owner that he wanted to return to the UK to see Helen and the boys and they parted on good terms. Brian and Keith packed their bags and they both flew back to England a couple of days later. Dave Shipley however decided to stay in South Africa and try to make a living there. Brian, like Helen was less than impressed by the white South Africans and wouldn't go back to South Africa.

Back to the North East

Dave Shipley's resignation from the trio left Brian without a bass player and so he and Keith took on a lad called Terry Betts but a few months later in 1972 Keith Patterson decided to join Andy Muat back in the butchery business at Ken Bells Butchers. It turned out that Dave Shipley hadn't been able to make a go of it in Africa and had returned to the North East and approached Brian with a view to rejoining. Brian agreed and although without a drummer he told Dave to get himself a guitar and that with Terry Betts on bass they would use club drummers wherever they got work. They worked like this for a few months until Terry Betts decided he wanted to leave and Brian looked around for a drummer. He found George Short who had worked with Brian some years previously when they auditioned for Decca in London but sadly he died very young and so Billy Lane from Brunswick became the trio's drummer.

Brian and Helen's youngest son Billy was born on 24th August 1972.

Billy Leonard

Billy hated school with a passion and Brian claims that he would take him to school through one door and Billy would be out the other in no time at all. However he was keen to work and whilst still at school he got a job on the milk, getting up at 3 or 4 o'clock in the morning and doing a milk round before (sometimes) going to school. On officially leaving school Billy joined the Royal Fleet Auxiliary which is a civilian-manned fleet of ships owned by the British Ministry of Defence and whose primary function is to supply the Royal Navy with fuel, ammunition and supplies, usually at sea. It also transports Army and Royal Marine personnel. His mother and father recall getting a message from Billy who was serving in the Gulf during the Gulf War to say that he had been injured. Not unnaturally Helen & Brian were anxious to find out what had happened only to learn from Billy that he'd been sitting in a deck chair, sunning himself, when it collapsed and pinched his finger in the frame! On leaving the RFA Billy got work in the factories in Cramlington, married Annabel and raised a family Curtis and Kelly.

The summer seasons of 1973 and 1974 saw the trio working at the Chuck Wagon Bar on Grand Parade in Skegness.

Butlins

Everything went well with the trio and in the summer of 1975 they got their first Butlins contract, 16 weeks in Pwllheli and because Billy Lane had a day job he gave way to John Siddle.

They enjoyed a great season at Butlins Pwllheli but unfortunately John's kidneys packed in and he had to receive dialysis treatment and as a result had to leave the band after a year. He was replaced on a temporary basis by Freddy Wilson. Everyone in the North East show business rallied round including the show band *The Millionaires* featuring Paul Squires, the comedian Alan Snell and many others and charity shows were organised and enough money was raised to get John Siddle his own dialysis machine in his back garden saving trips to the Royal Victoria Infirmary in Newcastle. Although he ultimately got a kidney transplant and resumed his playing career he subsequently relapsed, was hospitalised again and sadly John died in 2013.

John's illness obviously left the trio without a permanent drummer and as they had another season coming up at Butlins in the summer of 1976 Brian & Dave Shipley advertised for a replacement and auditioned drummers. One such hopeful was a 16 year old called David Herron from Blyth who was clearly the best but both Brian and Dave Shipley thought he looked far too young to play with two 'old codgers' like them. So a couple of days before they were due in Pwllheli Brian got in touch with his friend James Whale, at the time a late night phone-in chat show host at Metro Radio in Newcastle, who asked around but to no avail. James is now of course a better known broadcaster, radio presenter and paper reviewer on Sky TV News.

On the day they were due to leave for Pwllheli Brian said to Dave Shipley *"Go and get Davey Herron, I'll take the van with our gear and you bring Davey and his drum kit down in your car"*.

Davey Herron

David John Herron was born in Newcastle upon Tyne on the 15th March 1959 the son of Jack Herron and his wife Elsie and raised in the town of Blyth in South East Northumberland. Jack Herron worked as a plater in the Blyth shipyard subsequently obtaining a job at Swan Hunters in Wallsend, Tyneside where he worked on the building of the Esso Northumbria. The Esso Northumbria was the first of a series of very large crude oil carrier ships, built by Swans in 1968. When launched on 2 May 1969 by HRH Princess Anne she was the largest vessel to have been built in Britain at that time. The ship was designed to carry crude oil from the Persian Gulf, and its large design was a result of the Suez crisis in 1956, which had resulted in the closing of the Suez Canal. The ship was single-hulled and was designed with relatively limited knowledge of the behaviour of such large structures at sea, being generally a straightforward scaling up of a smaller design. It was also built to a fixed-price contract at a time when rampant inflation was occurring in Britain. This led to many attempts to cut costs for which Swan Hunter ultimately paid the price making a loss on the contract and its final cost being £6.5 million. Unfortunately the ship was plagued with problems both with its fittings and more seriously, with cracking of the hull under stress. It needed many repairs in its short working lifetime and this, together with fears of a major spill, prompted its retirement in 1982 after only 12 years in service. The ship was broken up at Kaohsiung, Taiwan.

David, better known as Davey, was a pupil at Morpeth Road Primary and Middle Schools and subsequently in Newlands Secondary Modern School which changed its name to Ridley High School whilst he was there. Ridley High was ultimately demolished in 2008 and the new Bede Academy built on the site in 2009 where coincidentally both Davey's children would become pupils. Davey left school with 6 CSEs (Certificate of Secondary Education) paradoxically neither of which was for music as he was a more technically minded student. Nevertheless the Herron family home had a musical influence as Davey's Mam Elsie was a pianist and organist as well as a singer and as he remembers there was always a piano or organ in the house. Elsie had begun her music career in concert parties playing the piano and became resident organist at the Bedlington Station club. She then worked in a number of clubs mainly in the Blyth

area but also in Bedlington, Morpeth and Ashington
and became the resident organist in the Canadian
lounge at the Coronation Club in Blyth.

Although not having excelled in music at school
Davey was fascinated with drumming and keen to
learn and had private lessons from the age of 11
including some with Tony, Brian's eldest son with
about 6 different drum teachers. Having been born
in 1959 Davey's musical taste was to be largely
influenced by the popular music of the 60s and the
development of the British rock scene and on into
the 1970's. Without a shadow of a doubt his favourite
band/singer has been *Roxy Music* and its front man
Bryan Ferry after he first heard their hit single
Virginia Plain in 1972. Davey has seen them perform
live many times both as a band and solo and met
Bryan Ferry personally.

On leaving school aged 15 Davey had a number of
jobs including kitchen work in a Chinese restaurant
in Blyth and peddling around town on a bike
delivering groceries for Walter Willsons, the grocery
chain that was once a familiar name on almost
every North-East High Street. His mother also got
him a job as drummer in the Canadian lounge of
the Coronation Club at the tender age of 15. Davey
also played at the Duke of Wellington Club in Blyth
and where, in 1976, he was resident when the call
came from Brian Leonard and Dave Shipley to join
the *Vance Clayton Trio*. Davey recalls being at his
grandmother's house when he answered a knock on

the door one Monday lunchtime and Dave Shipley saying *"Can you come to Butlins?"* *"When do you want me to go?"* replied Davey. *"NOW!"* said Dave Shipley.

So Davey had to quickly retrieve dirty laundry from the washing machine, pack bags and then go to the Duke of Wellington Club and explain why he was leaving and retrieve his drum kit. He and Dave Shipley then set off on the long journey to Pwllheli arriving at about 9pm that night and were actually on stage half an hour later.

Davey met his wife Anita from Cramlington and they were married on 20th November 1995 and they have two children Jack aged 18 and Melissa aged 16.

Illness

It was at Butlins in the summer season of 1976 that Brian, although continuing to perform, became unwell. He was feeling unusually tired, thirsty, losing weight and embarrassingly had a genital condition which was causing him some concern. He would regularly go to the camp doctor's surgery only to find it was a young lady doctor in attendance and too embarrassed to divulge his actual complaint would feign a sore throat!

Brian's wife Helen recalls that before setting off for his 16 week seasons she would buy him new clothes including shirts and jeans and that during that '76 season Brian would ring home and regularly complain that he was feeling unwell and that he was losing weight. The lads would often play football during their time off and Brian would tell her that after such exercise he was totally 'knackered', his clothes and jeans didn't fit anymore to such an extent that he was wearing some of young Davey's gear and that he had a genital infection which he was too embarrassed about to seek medical advice. Helen and her mother began scouring medical books and quickly came to the conclusion, when comparing his symptoms (unexplained weight loss, excessive thirst, feeling tired the entire time, genital itching etc) with certain medical conditions, that Brian had diabetes.

It was coming toward the end of the 16 weeks and because there was no way of contacting Brian directly (no mobile phones in those days) she rang the personnel officer at Butlins Pwllheli and asked to speak to Brian urgently. She told him go to the camp doctor immediately because he had diabetes. Brian saw the doctor, on this occasion a male, and was referred to Bangor hospital where they took blood tests and confirmed that he had indeed got Type 1 Diabetes and were amazed that, given his blood sugar content, he hadn't collapsed. Because of the physical exertion of performing on stage he was of course perspiring a great deal and this may have prevented him from passing out. He was prescribed medication and two weeks later at the end of the summer season he returned home and as she often jokingly did Helen asked *"Have you been good?"* and having prepared his manhood in advance by putting on a black condom Brian showed her and replied *"Still in its wrapper my dear!"*.

He spent a fortnight in the Royal Victoria Hospital during which time he & Helen were shown how to deal with the management of his condition including dietary control, blood sugar testing and insulin administration. Helen remembers having to practice by injecting oranges as a forerunner to Brian's anatomy!

She's done it ever since but it has never held him back from performing including one occasion at Christmas 2012 when he rang the Secretary of Dudley Senior Citizens' and Children's Treat Fund Charity on the morning of their fund raising Christmas Party at which he and Davey were booked to perform and informed him that he had been hospitalised the night before with hypoglycaemia (low blood sugar) but the duo would be there. They were and a great night was had by all.

Record Breakers

The summer of 1977 and the trio were back in Wales at Butlins holiday camp for their third consecutive and hugely successful season during which they had worked with some of show business' top stars of the time including Les Dennis, Frank Carson, Bob Monkhouse, Ken Dodd and *The Batchelors*. Although it was exceedingly rare for musicians and particularly groups to have more than two summer seasons as residents on the Butlins circuit the *Vance Clayton Trio* were by the summer of 1979 into their fifth residency at Pwllheli. In the 1970s most bars in Butlins' Holiday Centres had some sort of music and The Regency Bar in Pwllheli had by now become the 'home' of the *Vance Clayton Trio* and according to the camp's press officer at that time, Roger Woodcock, they had developed quite a following. According to him it used to be very quiet but was by then often difficult to get into and he claimed to know people who came just to listen to these three Geordie lads. They included many ladies who were mightily attracted by the trio and returned time and again but the record is claimed by a long time admirer of Brian a gentleman, now living in Port Isaac in Cornwall, who managed four weeks plus nine weekends in one 16 week season at Pwllheli just to listen to Brian. John Hilton and his partner Joyce still follow Brian by breaking their long summer vacations in Skegness and driving to the North East to listen to Brian & Davey at The Ship in Monkseaton and The Seahorse in Blyth a couple of times each year.

The trio's venue at Pwllheli was the Regency Bar where they played six nights and two afternoons a week. After the first few years as Roger Woodcock pointed out and as a result of their popularity the venue was increased in capacity and eventually seated some 1,500 people. The doors opened at 6:30pm and if one didn't get there early it was unlikely one would get a seat. Brian and the two lads took the stage at 7:30pm and were immaculately dressed in matching suits and shirts. Their opening signature tune was the John Paul Young hit "Love is in the air" and so it was as Brian stood behind his keyboards and dominated 'His Bar'. The trio would do several sets each night with a support act and/or Redcoat competitions between each set. In the 1970s hair styles were in fashion – the male curly mass perm was one and grey tints another – and the lads had to have them!

It is widely acknowledged that Geordies are particularly friendly and welcoming people and *Vance Clayton* certainly epitomised that when on stage and John Hilton recalls that Brian's followers at Butlins felt 'special' with him and the lads as he invited birthday or special occasion details which he read out and they played and sang to. Song requests too were encouraged and by the end of the evening the top of Brian's keyboard would be loaded with bits of paper and beer mats as folk piled on their favourites. Brian would also ensure that guests from various parts of the country and different nationalities were made to feel welcome by singing among other songs: 'We'll Keep A Welcome In The Hillside', 'When Irish Eyes Are Smiling', 'Maybe It's Because I'm A Londoner', 'The Jarrow Song' and 'Flower Of Scotland'. The Falklands War took place in the spring and early summer of 1982 and Brian ensured that tributes were paid to those young men and women fighting out there and was instrumental in organising charity collections for those killed and injured.

The trio's repertoire was phenomenal and considering there were few backing tapes and certainly no computers and mini disks in those days all the numbers they performed were committed to memory or sheet music. John Hilton compiled the following alphabetical list of about 180 songs that the *Vance Clayton Trio* performed at Butlins Pwllheli in just one week in the 1970s.

A

ALL ALONE

AMERICAN TRILOGY

ANNA MARIE

ANNIE'S SONG

APRIL SHOWERS

AQUARIUS

AS TIME GOES BY

B

BABY FACE

BANNER MAN

BEAUTIFUL DREAMER

BEATLES MELODY

BEGIN THE BEGUINE

BEN

BEST YEARS OF MY LIFE

BLUE BAYOU

BLUEBERRY HILL

BOY FROM NOWHERE

BRIDGE OVER TROUBLED WATER

BRIGHT EYES

C

CALIFORNIA

CAN'T SMILE WITHOUT YOU

CERTAIN SMILE

CHARMAINE

CHINA DOLL

COME ON OVER TO MY PLACE

COMING HOME

COVER OF THE ROLLING STONE

COWARD OF THE COUNTY

CRACKLIN' ROSE

D

DADDY DON'T YOU WALK

DANNY BOY

DAY WE WENT TO BANGO

RDAYTIME FRIENDS

DESPERADO

DISTANT DRUMS

DREAM

DRIFTERS MEDLEY

DRUM SOLO (WIPEOUT)

E

EVEN NOW

EVERGREEN

EVERYTHING I OWN

F

FEELINGS

FLOWER OF SCOTLAND

FOR ALL WE KNOW

FOR ME AND MY GIRL

FOR THE GOOD TIMES

FUNNY FAMILIAR

FRIDAY NIGHT

G

GREATEST LOVE OF ALL

GREAT PRETENDER

GREEN GREEN GRASS OF HOME

GONNA BE STRONG

H

HALFWAY TO PARADISE

HAPPY ATMOSPHERE

HAWAIIAN WED SONG

HELLO

HELLO MY FRIEND

HELP ME MAKE IT

HEY JUDE

HONEY

HOT AUGUST NIGHT

HOUSE OF THE RISING SUN

HOW DO YOU DO IT

HUNGRY YEARS

HURT

I

I BEG YOUR PARDON

I CAN'T STOP LOVING YOU

I JUST CALLED TO SAY I LOVE YOU

I MADE IT THROUGH THE RAIN

I WON'T FORGET YOU

I WRITE THE SONGS

IF

IF YOU KNEW SUSIE

I'LL PUT YOU TOGETHER

I'LL TAKE YOU HOME AGAIN

IN YOUR EYES

I'M GONNA LOVE YOU

I'M ON MY WAY

IMAGINE

IN DREAMS

IT FEELS LIKE I'M IN LOVE

IT'S ONLY MAKE BELIEVE

J

JARROW SONG

JERUSALEM

JUST THE WAY YOU ARE

JUST TO HAVE YOU BACK

K

KELLY

KILLARNEY

L

LAST FAREWELL

LATELY

LIVING ALL RIGHT

LONG & WINDING TRAIL

LOVE IS ALL

LOVE IS IN THE AIR

LOVE ON THE ROCKS

LOVE STORY

LOVING YOU

LUCILLE

LYING EYES

M

MAGGIE

MAKING IT BIG

MAMMY

MATCHSTICK MEN

MAY EACH DAY OF THE WEEK

MEMORIES

MIDNIGHT

MISS YOU NIGHTS

MISTY

MULL OF KINTYRE

MY BEST FRIEND

MY PRAYER

MY WAY

O

ONCE IN AWHILE

ONE DAY AT A TIME

ONLY THE LONELY

ONLY YOU

OO BLA DI OO BLA DA

P

PAL OF MY CRADLE DAYS

PAT BOONE MEDLEY

POWER OF LOVE

PRETTY WOMAN

R

RAMBLING ROSE

RAMONA

RED RED ROBIN

RED RED WINE

RELEASE ME

ROCKING ALL OVER

ROW THE BOAT

RUNAWAY

RUNNINGBEAR

S

SAILING

SAILING IN WINDS

SAY YOU'LL STAY 'TIL TOMORROW

SEA OF HEARTBREAK

SHE BELIEVES IN ME

SO SAD

SOLITAIRE

SOMETIMES WHEN WE KISS

SOMETHING STUPID

STAY

STILL

SUMMER HOLIDAY

SUNSHINE OF YOUR SMILE

SUSPICIOUS MINDS

SWEET CAROLINE

T

TAKE GOOD CARE OF MY BABY

TEENAGER IN LOVE

THE MUSIC MAN

THIS IS OUR LOVELY DAY

THIS OLD HOUSE

THREE STEPS TO HEAVEN

THREE TIMES A LADY

TILL

TOO SOON TO KNOW

TRULY

TRUMPINGTON

TWELFTH OF NEVER

U

UNCHAINED MELODY

UP WHERE WE BELONG

UP TOWN GIRL

W

WAKE UP MAGGIE

WANT TO WAKE UP

WAY ON DOWN

WAY WE WERE

WE ARE THE WORLD

WE DON'T TALK ANYMORE

WELCOME HOME

WE'LL KEEP A WELCOME

WHEN I FALL IN LOVE

WHEN I GROW TOO OLD

WHISPERING GRASS

WHITER SHADE OF PALE

WILLIAM TELL

WITH THESE HANDS

WONDER OF YOU

WORDS

Y

YOU LOOK WONDERFUL

YOU NEEDED ME

YOU'RE THE ONLY GOOD THING

YOUR SONG

One of John's favourite songs was Kelly and his
daughter, now in her early 40s, was named after it.
It is also one of Brian's best loved numbers which he
still performs today and one of his granddaughters is
of course also named Kelly.

In front of the stage in the Regency Bar at Pwllheli lay a narrow strip of carpet used for dancing and Brian would encourage folk to *'let their hair down'* and do 'Shakin' Stevens, 'Row The Boat' or the 'Trumpington' dance. Later in the evening he would have people snaking around the entire bar doing the Conga!

The highlight of the trio's act was indeed a strange one when at the end of the evening they would finish with the same two numbers, the first of which Brian pioneered and many acts subsequently adopted. In his unique version of 'The Music Man' Brian introduced verses using the 'Match of The Day' theme tune, 'The Dam Busters' film score and 'Benny' from Crossroads and so on and during which he encouraged holiday makers to act out and dance. For the finale the trio would play and Brian would sing the old Women's Institute hymn 'Jerusalem'. The effect on the audience was shattering and by the end of the opening bars just about everyone in the, by now, crowded bar was standing on tables and chairs – arms in the air – waiting to sing the words. Spontaneously – from handbags or elsewhere – items of women's underwear including knickers, bras and suspender belts would appear and waved in the air in time with the music. Even when they finished the audience would carry on singing the hymn as they made their way down the chalet lines to their beds. In 1979 the camp press officer Roger Woodcock added *"Over 200,000 people must have listened to these three lads in the past four years – a splendid tribute to their high standard and their pleasant personalities".*

The trio's day off was Sunday and they would regularly go horse riding on the beaches and Brian of course would like to follow his hobby of golf at either the Pwllheli Golf Club or along the coast at Criccieth, where amongst others he played with *The Batchelors*, Les Dennis, Frank Carson and Mike Reid who were also appearing at Butlins as cabaret artistes.

Back in 1881 Gladstone's Liberal government, sponsored by prominent Welsh non-conformists in the Liberal party including the future Prime Minister David Lloyd George, passed The Sunday Closing (Wales) Act 1881 banning the sale of alcohol on the Sabbath. It would not be repealed until 1961, when each county was charged with holding a referendum on Sunday opening, to gauge support in their particular area. Pwllheli as part of a mainly rural and Welsh speaking county therefore maintained its dry-Sunday status and so it was when the trio were playing at Butlins in the '70s although private clubs could get exemption. Pwllheli Conservative Club was therefore packed on a Sunday night and even more so when Brian and the lads would make a guest appearance.

Barry Redman had by this time taken over as guitarist from Alan Roberts who had been with the trio for a few years. Alan had also got a job with the Council and although telling his employer that he was going to Australia to visit relatives and thereby given 4 weeks leave of absence he had to leave the trio mid-season and Barry replaced him.

Practical Jokes

Practical jokes were often played on Brian and the lads and it was not uncommon for someone to surreptitiously enter their dressing room, at the side of the stage, and for the lads to find a shirt or other item of clothing missing. Yet there it was stuck to the ceiling of the Regency Bar where it remained all season. The culprit was never found and how they managed to do it will never be known. Then there was the mischief maker who discovered where Brian's chalet, which he shared with Davey Herron, was situated. Most visitors to Butlins in those days knew how to gain access to the chalets by prising open the window, putting a hand through to the adjacent door knob and gaining entry! The miscreant in this case took a donkey from the donkey compound in the fairground, led the hapless beast through the chalet lines and pushed it into Brian's chalet whilst he was still on stage of course before removing the light bulb! The donkey had predictably 'performed its business' all over the floor which Brian had to clean up. Lo and behold the following night Davey & Brian returned to the chalet after midnight full of beer to find what Brian thought was a rat leaping about under the covers in his bed! Brian pulled back the sheet and found the ugliest looking fish – a catfish – writhing around in the bed. Between them they managed to get the creature into a black bin bag and took it to the nearby duck pond where it remained for some weeks living on newly hatched ducklings! It transpired that this was all the work of Freddie Smith the head waiter on the camp. Freddie, a scouser, was a likeable rogue who would keep Brian and the lads well stocked with provisions particularly when Helen was down with the boys on holiday.

Expecting a similar practical joke the trio were playing in the Regency Bar when a young lass by the name of Dixie who would get up and sing the Connie Francis hit 'Stupid Cupid' came rushing up to the front of the stage shouting *"Brian, Brian do you know your chalet's on fire!!!"*. *"Don't be daft"* Brian replied *"just do Stupid Cupid if you want to sing a song"*. Breathless she shouted back *"No, no your chalet really is on fire and there are fire engines and everything there!"* Barry Redman told Brian he would leave the stage and go and have a look. When he came back he told Brian that not only had his chalet burned down but the chalet above and the one next door as well! *"I think we're in for some tough shit in the morning"* commented Barry. It transpired that because Brian had set up a number of tape machines recording the trio's songs for sale in the Regency Bar, one had overheated and caught fire in turn setting fire to the chip pan and the rest of the chalet's contents. Whilst sifting through the debris after the fire Brian, who's colour blind, held up a badly scorched item of clothing and mockingly shouted to Davey Herron *"Look Davey here's your green Le Breve shirt"* to which Davey replied *"It's not my green one Brian it's your blue one!"*

The next morning Brian was called into the office by the camp hierarchy and told *"Do you realise that you've set fire to your chalet and caused nearly fifty thousand pounds worth of damage?"* Brian looked at them and said *"I could've burnt the whole bloody camp down and not done that much damage!"* to which they all fell about laughing and told him to push off. As he was leaving he poked his head round the door and enquired *"Any chance of another chalet please?"*

Another amusing story Brian tells involved his friend Tommy Dowson, the drummer from High Pit Club in Cramlington, who was paying a brief visit to see Brian and the lads at Butlins. They had had a good night and were on their way back to the chalet when Brian got his eye on a comedian from Liverpool (no names – no pack drill), who was also working at the camp, with a well known 'lady of ill repute' in the shadows. *"I'm only talking to the lass"* shouted the comic. *"Aye well that's alright then!"* replied Brian laughing as he and Tommy continued on their way. Brian had a double bed and as it was only one night that Tommy was staying he agreed to share it with him. As he got ready for bed Tommy pointed out to Brian that his girlfriend back home had painted his toenails bright red whilst he was asleep the night before and he couldn't get it off. Just then there was a knock at the door and Brian opened it to find the Scouse comic stood there. *"Clayton you're gonna tell everyone I've been with that lass"* exclaimed the comic as he took one look at Tommy laying there with his painted toenails and continued *"Eh! - look at his feet*

he's wearing nail varnish and you're sleeping with him –
you're saying nought about me Clayton!!!"

Davey Herron was also the target for the practical
jokes and recalls one occasion when the trio were
performing *The Surfaris* 1963 rock classic 'Wipe
Out' and he was left on stage performing the drum
solo that Ron Wilson, *The Surfaris'* drummer, had
perfected and every aspiring young drummer in
bands tried to emulate. Unbeknown to Davey a
Butlins Redcoat had locked Brian and the guitarist
Barry Redman in the dressing room and he was left
on stage sweating profusely and eventually threw
his sticks in the air, shrugged his shoulders at the
audience and went to find the other two lads. On
another occasion he had his drum sticks smothered
in butter by some wag! Holiday camps in the 1960s,
1970s and 1980s were without doubt vastly different
from today's holiday entertainment centres.

For Brian of course it didn't end then as, although
with changes in personnel, the *Vance Clayton Trio*
with Brian always at the helm continued at Butlins
until 1995 and in so doing found their way into the
Butlins' record book as their longest serving trio.
They were the last of Butlins' resident bands and
some would say the camps have never been the same.
During the two decades the trio had performed
alongside or backed many stars of the day including
Frank Ifield, Norman Collier, Lulu, *The Beverley
Sisters*, Rod Hull & Emu, Vince Earl, Mike Reid and
the Geordie comedy duo *Lambert & Ross* to name but

a few. The stars would appear as the cabaret spot at midnight and the trio were contracted and paid to support or back them in a two hour slot from midnight until 2am and any longer was therefore paid as overtime at double or treble time rates. Ken Dodd was a regular at Butlins in those days and a big hit with the lads as he would regularly overrun and sometimes it would be 4 o'clock in the morning before he came off. They hadn't had to work too much either as Ken would do his stand-up routine for most of the time and they only had to play when he sang a few numbers or brought on the *Diddymen*. The entertainments manager would 'do his nut' when the trio's timesheets went in!

In the seventies Butlins also hosted other big names from the wider world of entertainment including snooker stars, one of whom was Jim Meadowcroft who would appear in the Spanish Bar at Pwllheli. At about that time Jim was ranked number 12 in the World Snooker rankings and would be a regular in the audience to listen to Brian and the lads and over time became their friend and along with Vince Earl would join them for drinks in the lads' dressing room. Vince 'Mark' Earl was a regular at Pwllheli, coming as he did from the Liverpool area, and he and Brian became friends and would join the trio on their impromptu performances at the Pwllheli Conservative Club on a Sunday night. Vince had started his career in the Merseybeat scene of the 1960s as the singer with *Vince Earl Talisman* and *Vince Earl & The Attractions* and later played in the band

Rory Storm and the Hurricanes. He became a stand up comedian in the TV show The Comedians and went on to star in the TV soap opera Brookside. In 2010 Vince was diagnosed with Goodpasture's Syndrome, an acute autoimmune disease which attacks the lungs and kidneys leading to kidney failure and the need for regular dialysis. In the summer of 2012 he underwent a successful kidney transplant.

Life on the road wasn't all *'beer and skittles'* for Brian and the lads and was even tougher on their families. Nonetheless Brian's wife Helen recollects that she always coped even when he was some 6,000 miles away in Africa and she was living with their two boys in Whickham they regularly exchanged letters and the occasional phone call when he got the opportunity to speak to Tony and Paul. Her mother and father would baby sit once a month and Heather, Dave Shipley's wife, and Helen would have a night out at La Strada a night club in Sunderland owned by the agency Beverley Artists who Brian had worked for for many years. During the school holidays and when Brian was working at Butlins Helen and the boys would travel to Pwllheli and be a family again and when not together they had a snooker table in the house for winter months and wet days and Tony, Paul and Billy were all mad keen on sports during summer and fine weather. Throughout their marriage and notwithstanding Brian's professional career Helen & Brian have enjoyed a loving and content relationship based on mutual trust. Even though the very nature of his chosen profession and his good looks attracted many female admirers Helen never doubted him and knew that he always loved her and the boys. They squabbled like all couples do but, in Helen's words *"affairs on either side would have ended the marriage"*. She was and remains his loving wife, trusted confidante and nurse. Assessing his sugar levels and insulin requirements for his diabetes and managing and administering all his other medication for his other medical conditions including asthma, rheumatoid arthritis and Crohn's disease which was diagnosed in 2000. Crohn's disease is one type of inflammatory bowel disease for which there is no known pharmaceutical or surgical cure. Treatment options are restricted to controlling symptoms with medication, lifestyle and dietary changes, maintaining remission and preventing relapse.

Summertime was by now taken up with their work at Butlins but out of season the trio continued to ply their trade around the pubs, clubs and entertainment venues largely in the North East of England where their reputation ensured large and enthusiastic audiences. In 1978 the *Vance Clayton Trio* joined the tremendously successful show – *The Dixielanders Music Hall* – at White Mare Pool in Felling where they stood in for entertainers taking holidays or other engagements.

DAVEY HERRON – BRIAN – DAVE
SHIPLEY, BUTLINS, PWLLHELI

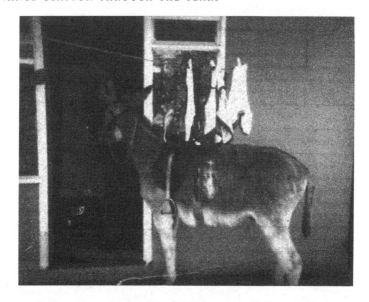

**DONKEY BEING LED INTO BRIAN'S
CHALET BY FREDDIE SMITH**

THE JERUSALEM FINALE

DAVEY HERRON – VINCE EARL – TONY LEONARD
– BARRY REDMAN & A COUPLE OF REDCOATS

Though based on a great Geordie entertainment
tradition it was quite innovative in its day when two
local comedians, Bobby Hooper and Billy Martin
established the venue in the former White Mare Pool
Hotel in the 1970s. It was an instant success and
certainly one of the top venues to visit for comedy,
music, food and drink and visitors had to book
months in advance and then queue to get in. At that
time the trio worked with some of the best known
and loved local artistes including Alan Fox, Cindy
Kelly, Brian Lewis, Larry Mason, Terry Millican, Alan
Snell, Rebecca Storm, Bobby (The Little Waster)
Thompson and of course the resident hosts at the
Dixielanders Bobby Hooper and Billy Martin.

Having recently been awarded a silver disc from their recording company Impulse Studios for their LP 'The Way We Were', the trio were invited to join forces with the Dixielanders to appear in a new Geordie night out in Sunderland on a contract for 6 nights a week at Roker Park. The Dixielanders Music Hall had taken over Sunderland Football Club's Roker Function Suite, Brooks night club and the Jack Parker restaurant. The trio were joined by North East comics Alan Fox and Alan Snell, the singers Cindy Kelly and Rebecca Storm and compere Larry Mason.

In 1978 Brian was working for the Beverley Artists agency and a police officer recently transferred from High Spen to Whickham Police Station was asked to take on the station's entertainment secretary's role and approached the agency for entertainment suggestions. The *Vance Clayton Trio* was proposed and thus began a long association and friendship between Brian and Jeff Wanless, the police officer, which has lasted to this day. Jeff and his wife Sylvia were regulars at the gigs Brian did and not just for the police force but at other clubs and pubs around the North East and soon became friends with Brian and Helen and holidayed with them.

By 1979 Spanish City, the funfair in Whitley Bay immortalised by Mark Knopfler and *Dire Straits* in their 1981 single 'Tunnel of Love', had converted its Rotunda into the Starlight Rooms staging live entertainment. The person responsible for booking such entertainment was Alan Morris and the *Vance*

Clayton Trio was one of his first choices. As a result Alan formed a business relationship with Brian and like Jeff a friendship which has lasted for over 25 years. Alan continued to book Brian as he moved on from the Starlight Rooms to become landlord at The Pheasant, steward at Arcot Hall Golf Club and now Centre Manager at Preston Grange Community Centre where Brian and Davey are regularly invited to perform as the *Vance Clayton Duo*.

Brian has occasion to remember, with a degree of embarrassment, when he, Helen, Jeff Wanless and his wife Sylvia were on holiday in Tenerife, in fact Brian & Helen's first on the island and staying in Los Cristianos in Alan Morris' apartment. After their arrival Helen was busy unpacking their luggage and Brian went out onto the balcony in a pair of shorts and fell asleep in the sun and of course got badly burned on his head and shoulders. The following day whilst Helen, Jeff and Sylvia went to the roof pool Brian went for a cold beer in the April Fool Bar in the pub below. He sat there alone when an elderly gentleman came in with his glass of whisky and asked Brian if he could join him. *"I'm Matt"* he said and Brian introduced himself and they engaged in conversation with Brian telling the other guy about his music career. They chatted for a couple of hours and Brian told him that he was appearing at a night club up the road that very evening and Matt asked if he could tag along with his female companion to which Brian readily agreed.

By this juncture Brian realised that he had run up quite a bar bill and called up to Helen to send some cash down. Jeff Wanless came with the money and as he entered the bar he saw the elderly gentleman and immediately said *"Hello Matt lovely to see you"*. Brian was startled by that and asked Jeff how he knew him. *"It's MATT BUSBY you barmy bugger!"* retorted Jeff and Brian apologised profusely to Sir Matt and related how he'd been rambling on and on about his music and hadn't realised who he was. Sir Matt told Brian not to worry and how much he had enjoyed talking to him about music and especially as he hadn't recognised him nor had wanted to talk about football. He and his lady friend went along that night and joined Brian's company and had a great time. They met up again the following day for a drink but unfortunately someone stole Sir Matt's companion's handbag and they had to change the locks on their apartment. They continued to meet up during the holiday and Brian recalls how pleased he was to have met such a lovely man. Sir Alexander Matthew "Matt" Busby, CBE, KCSG died not long after that holiday of cancer, aged 84, in January 1994 in Cheadle Manchester. For many of the intervening years Jeff helped Brian with his gear when attending functions at which Brian was playing and following Brian's stroke a couple of years ago now reads out the quiz questions for Clayton's Quiz at The Seahorse in Blyth every Wednesday night when he and his wife Sylvia attend.

ROKER PARK MUSIC HALL BILLING

JEFF WANLESS – SIR MATT BUSBY – BRIAN, TENERIFE

135

Working men's clubs and concert chairmen

In 1862 The Rev. Henry Solly founded the Club and Institute Union Limited (CIU) or Working Men's Club and Institute Union Limited as it is known today. He was an important activist in the campaign for the extension of working class political rights and also helped to set up the Charity Organisation Society. Nevertheless the established CIU was, and still remains, non-political although individual clubs can be and are affiliated to political parties. In the pre- and post-World War I era these clubs were often associated with trade societies and trade union branches and more recently in the miners' strike of the early 1980s, the Miners' Welfare Clubs were prominent in their support of the strike. Socialist Clubs were built before the establishment of the Labour Party but as the party grew in size in the 1920s Labour clubs were founded. Generally, Conservative clubs did not join as they formed their own federation although there are some. Other such clubs can be recognised by their title e.g. Engineers or Railwaymen's Clubs.

Servicemen returning from the Great War would also establish Ex-Servicemen's clubs and Roman Catholic Church parishes too had their own. The only stipulation demanded for membership of the CIU was that clubs be owned by the members and accepted the standards of membership.

Originally it was a middle-class led benevolent organisation aimed at education and non-alcoholic recreation. Nonetheless working men themselves soon took over the running of the CIU and drinks were allowed to be consumed in the clubs' premises. In 1919, thirteen working men's clubs in the north-east of England formed an independent co-operative to supply their own beer and the Northern Clubs' Federation brewery was established. Until its closure in 2004 the brewery, coincidentally situated off Wellington Road in Dunston where the Leonards had once lived, was still owned and run by its 303 member clubs. Federation Ordinary and Federation Special were their most popular draught beers and supplies were delivered to the House of Commons in Westminster for nearly forty years to satisfy North East MPs.

Arguably, it could be said that working men's clubs have suffered from an old-fashioned image among young people and have found it hard to compete with modern trends, resulting in the closure of vast numbers of CIU affiliated clubs in recent years.

Many entertainers cut their teeth and developed their skills in CIU clubs around the country over the years and in particular in the North East. One such entertainer was a comedian called Norman Collier who, although born and bred in Hull plied his trade during the 1960s in the wider northern working men's club circuit and was a regular in the North East. He and Brian became good friends and he regularly stayed with Brian & Helen in Eastfield Green, Cramlington when he was working locally and had their kids rolling around the floor with his chicken antics. Their friendship started in the seventies when the Beverley Artists Agency booked Norman for a season in the North East performing at social clubs all over the region. The show consisted of Norman, a singer from Blackpool called Wendy Kay and the *Vance Clayton Trio* with Brian, Keith Patterson and Dave Shipley. His act was based on the time-honoured northern comic school and involved non-racist situational monologues as opposed to a series of jokes. He is probably best known for two classic routines: one in the guise of a traditional working men's club compere with a faulty microphone and the other imitating a chicken with its noises and gestures. Brian recalls lying in a ward in the Royal Victoria Hospital in Newcastle following diagnosis of his diabetes earlier at Butlins feeling very sorry for himself when the ward suddenly erupted into hysterics as Norman Collier arrived to visit Brian performing his chicken routine.

Brian also recollects Miles Knox opening a night club in South Shields called Rum Runner when he invited Norman Collier and the trio to the opening by the famous racehorse Red Rum. Red Rum was led in and promptly defecated all over the new carpet. Fortunately there was time for the staff to clean up before the punters arrived. Brian and Norman met up on many occasions and in particular when they were both working at Butlins. Brian would frequently invite bands, singers and comics back to his chalet where he had prepared massive curries. One night just as everyone was leaving a paramedic was called to the chalet line to attend someone who had had a heart attack. Norman had already left but about a quarter of an hour later there was a knock on the door and there he was standing having come all the way back down the chalet line and said *"It must've been the curry Brian!"* and promptly walked off!

Norman died on 14th March 2013 aged 87 after a long battle with Parkinson's disease. Stars from the world of comedy paid their last respects to Norman along with his wife Lucy of more than 60 years and their family at his funeral in Welton, East Yorkshire on 27th March 2013. Russ Abbott, Syd Little, Eddie Large, Bobby Ball, Roy "Chubby" Brown, Tom O'Connor, Roy Hudd and Roy Walker joined hundreds of people as his coffin was carried into St Helen's church to the sound of a trumpeter playing 'From This Moment On', from Kiss Me Kate - the tune Norman Collier came on stage to during his long career. Unfortunately Brian was unable to attend as he was recovering from a bout of bronchitis.

In 1974 Granada Television produced a variety show set in a fictional workingmen's club in the North of England entitled The Wheeltappers and Shunters Social Club which quite brilliantly characterised the real thing and followed their earlier run called The Comedians. The series Wheeltappers and Shunters ran for 3 years and featured many acts regularly seen on the Northern CIU club circuits including those who were reaching the end of their popularity, like the 50's crooner *Johnnie Ray*. It also gave acts such as *Cannon & Ball*, *The Dooleys* and magician Paul Daniels their first TV exposure. Other artists to appear on the show included singers Kathy Kirby, Roy Orbison, Buddy Greco, Nana Mouskouri, Freddie Garrity, Karl Denver, *The Three Degrees*, and *The Batchelors* and entertainers and musicians George Melly, Tessie O'Shea and Lonnie Donegan together with comedians Bernard Manning, George Roper, Jim Bowen and Frank Carson.

The show was hosted by the Wheeltappers & Shunters Social Club 'chairman', the comedian Colin Crompton who routinely rang his hand-cranked fire alarm bell and called for the live audience to *"giv' us some order now"* and between acts made announcements from *"the Committee"*. That routine had of course been pioneered by Norman Collier.

Colin played stooge to the Social Club's compere (better known in the North East as the 'concert chairman') and realistically portrayed by Bernard Manning who later claimed that he was given the role because he had that gaumless look about him which made him ideal for the part.

Brian Leonard recalls several such characters in clubs where he played over the years and who gave rise to humorous incidents – not all of them politically correct by today's standards. He remembers one night when the band were setting up their gear with 12 spot lights at the front of the stage and two banks of 3 spot lights behind them in Chirton Social Club in North Shields. The concert chairman came up and said *"I see you've got your own lights lads!"*, *"That's good"* he said, *"it'll save our electricity!!!"*

Another such occasion occurred in High Pit Club in Cramlington where Brian and the band were playing at a darts presentation night and it was brought up at the Club's Committee meeting that they were going to fill the trophies (cups) with pints of beer although one committee man had suggested that they save a bit of money by *'filling them with halves!'*

At the same club one Saturday night there was a spectacular and the *Vance Clayton Trio* were booked with a comedian called Oliver along with the star attraction from America *The Drifters*. The trio and the comedian had completed their spots in the show and it was time for the top of the bill when Ronnie Cliff, the concert chairman, said *"Ladies and Gentlemen just before we bring the main turn on I'd just like to mention that in the boxing tonight Barry McGuigan knacked the darkie! Will you please put your hands together and welcome on stage the fabulous Drifters"*. When the stage curtains opened apparently *The Drifters* were laying all over the stage laughing and could barely do their first number.

The concert chairman at Throckley Union Jack club was a lad called Joe Jobling who had the nickname

141

Pay 'Em Off Joe because if he didn't like the act he would go up to him and say *"Get yersel' a bottle o' broon te tek oot bonny lad"*. He would then announce to the audience *"Sorry but the torn's not ower cliver – he's had te gan hyem!"* Brian was only too pleased that his band was Joe's favourite as he would turn to Brian and say *"Howway Clayton dee another spot hinny"*.

During the 1970s working men's clubs in the North East held Sunday afternoon striptease shows when Brian and the lads would often do a cabaret spot. One such popular venue for these shows was Wallsend Miners Welfare where the trio would open the show and be heckled by the audience to shouts of *"get 'em off and get the strippers on!"* One Sunday Brian recalls waiting in the dressing room where a young stripper was breast feeding a baby and asked him to wind the bairn whilst she went on and did her act. Brian held the baby on his shoulder and patted its back until the lass came off stage and said she would put him on the other breast before she rushed off to another gig at a club down the road.

Johnny Hammond was a comedian and comic script writer who hailed originally from Hartlepool and was a winner of television's New Faces competition, and appeared at the London Palladium several times and wrote material for Jim Davidson, *Hale and Pace* and Roy 'Chubby' Brown. Brian remembers being booked to appear with Johnny and a female singer at the Downhill Club in Sunderland. After setting up their gear they were all waiting to go on stage when having looked through the curtains, they saw a lad sat in the audience with a shotgun and everyone started to panic. The management of the club asked everyone to stay calm and carry on as usual but the singer refused to go on so Johnny Hammond stepped forward and said *"I die on my arse anyway, I'll go on"* which he did and launched into his routine cracking jokes, singing and playing the piano out of tune in the style of Les Dawson. During his act plain clothes policemen came in, disarmed and arrested the guy with the shotgun and dragged him to the concert room door at which point Johnny Hammond called out *"Can you come back and get the rest of the bastards please!"*

One of Brian's agents during his career in the 70s was the Wansbeck Theatrical Agency in Bedlington with Hughie and Ian Turner and George Maclean. On one occasion Brian had just returned from Tenerife on holiday when he learned that Hughie Turner had died. He found out that Johnny Hammond had rung the agency a couple of days after Hughie's death and spoken to his widow Edythe saying that he had just heard that he had died and was it true. He offered his condolences and put the phone down only to ring back five minutes later and spoke again with Edythe and said *"It's me, it's Johnny again - he is definitely dead isn't he?"* *"Oh yes Johnny"* she replied *"he passed away three days ago"*. *"Well you know what a lying bastard he really was?"* quipped Johnny Hammond. Apparently when Edythe related the story to the rest of the agency team in the office they all fell about laughing and it really relieved some of the atmosphere. Johnny Hammond died of cancer in 2007 and his autobiography, self deprecatingly entitled, The Art of Dying was published the following year.

As many people in a variety of professions have had to do and in order to secure profitable work the trio of Brian, Dave Shipley and Keith Patterson would spend a great deal of time away from home leaving their wives and families for considerable periods. One such occasion they obtained a cabaret engagement in the Broadway Club in Manchester for an impresario called Bunny Lewis who was also a drag artist. The trio were booked to play at a working men's club in the evening and then on to the Broadway for the midnight cabaret. The show comprised an Australian singer who topped the bill, a girl singer and *Cannon & Ball* who hadn't at that time become very well known and of course the *Vance Clayton Trio*.

That week the trio stayed with Bunny Lewis at his house and although he only had two bedrooms he offered to put up a couple of exotic dancers he had also booked for a night. He told the girls that he would provide extra beds and they could either stay with Brian, Dave and Keith in their bedroom or join him in his. Eying the three randy Geordies it wasn't a difficult choice for the lasses, or so they thought and they opted to spend the night in Bunny's bedroom. They found out that he wasn't the homosexual they thought he was and he had them both!

Bunny Lewis told the trio that on the Thursday night
he had booked a female singer from America to do
the early evening show but tickets weren't selling
very well and he had cancelled the trio's booking at
another club but wanted them to have the evening
off and join the audience. Brian asked who it was
and Bunny told him it was none other than Sarah
Vaughan the jazz singer! The lads got front row
seats in time to see her backing band – piano, bass
and drums - set up and play a couple of opening
numbers. The compere introduced Sarah Vaughan
and Brian said the hairs on his arms stood up as
she entertained as if there was a thousand strong
audience. They couldn't believe there were only about
sixty or seventy people in the room to listen to one
of the world's greatest jazz artists. She proceeded
to tell the audience that she'd only ever had one hit
in the UK – 'Passing Strangers' – which she had
duetted with a man. She went on to say that it just
so happened that that very gentleman was there in
the audience sitting amongst them and was sure he
would sing along from where he was. With that the
spotlight swung around to just behind where the
lads were sitting and fell on Billy Eckstine. Sarah
Vaughan moved to the edge of the stage without her
microphone and broke into the song and sure enough
Billy Eckstine joined in. Brian said it was absolutely
fabulous and a night he will never easily forget.

The *Vance Clayton Trio* also travelled to Swansea in
South Wales to appear in cabaret at the Townsman
Club where they supported Paul Melba the comedy

impressionist and the venue had a band called the *Townsman Band* fronted by Bonny Tyler. The lads also appeared a number of times at Bernard Manning's Embassy Club in Manchester. Bernard Manning was well known among the comedy fraternity for 'pinching' their jokes, as Roy Walker will attest, but did a lot of charity work and as a good friend of George Maclean raised a lot of money for charity at High Pit Club in its heyday.

Manchester City Supporters Club was another venue where the trio were booked for a week long engagement in the early 70s with the Nolan family – *The Singing Nolans* - father Tommy, mother Maureen, sons Tommy and Brian and five daughters Anne, Denise, Maureen, Linda and Bernadette. Hailing originally from Dublin they were of course Irish and devout Roman Catholics. The trio opened the show and to use Brian's own words *"We died on our arses!"* - partly one assumes because they were Geordies in a Manchester City supporters club but principally because the audience were there to see the Nolans. The family went down a storm and the following day Brian observed that a Catholic priest would attend on the family and bless all the kids. As he passed the trio's dressing room Brian called him over and said *"Any chance of blessing us Father?" "Are you Catholics?"* replied the priest. *"No we're not even religious but the Nolans are doing great and we're dying a death and wondered if a blessing for us might help?"* The priest took it in good spirits and left the building laughing.

The trio worked in Birmingham for the Bernard Parr agency who booked them for a tour of the local clubs. Bernie Burgess ran the agency and was married to Ruby Murray the Irish singer who had been very popular in the UK and Ireland in the 1950s having had nine UK Top 10 hit singles including 'Softly, Softly' and 'Let Me Go Lover'. He was also her manager and booked the *Vance Clayton Trio* to back her at a Birmingham venue. Brian recalls that although her voice was unique it was extremely timid and quiet consequently he had to play very quietly and ramp up the amplifier for her microphone. She passed away in Torquay in December 1996 aged only 61 but her name lives on, curiously, in rhyming slang for curry!

After Dave Shipley left the group and Billy Lane had joined the trio they toured Scotland and worked one night with *The Alexander Brothers* (Tom & Jack) in Glasgow's Metropole Theatre. The brothers outsold the Beatles in the 1960s north of the border with their hit single 'Nobody's Child'.

Agents

Brian had a number of agents over the years starting with the Jack Wright Agency in Newcastle who booked him for The Vine Grill. He then joined the Top Class Agency run by Brian Shelley and Bart Elliott in Sunderland for one year. The Beverley Agency in South Shields operated by Bob Deplidge, Bill Reeves and later Bob Gladwyn became his third agents. Bill Reeves, who had been a cameraman for Tyne Tees television and a singer who performed with the Vance Claytons as well as solo, took Brian on and managed him and Bob Deplidge left shortly after and was replaced by Ralph Philips. The Beverley Agency booked hundreds of acts but only two groups, The Vance Claytons and an Irish showband called *The 3 Days* comprising three brothers Adrian, Charlie, and Michael Douglas. Being the only two groups employed by the agency they all got on well together and became good friends. Adrian later formed a country & western singing duo with Patsy Nolan and Charlie and Michael went their own ways and on to become top comics - Charlie winning Opportunity Knocks with the stage name Charlie Daze and Michael with the stage name of Mike Cash winning New Faces. Charlie is now semi-retired and living in Jersey and Mike is still pulling in audiences nation-wide with his Irish wit and charm.

Beverley Agency also looked after a number of the North East clubs' favourite comedians including Bobby Knoxall and Walter Gee. Bobby Knoxall was the stage name of Robert McKenna who was born in the East End of Sunderland in 1933 and after being expelled from school at the age of 12 got a job selling fruit from a barrow. It all began for Bobby aged 16 when he was working as a pot man (collecting glasses) in a Sunderland pub when he asked the landlord if he could sing. Patrons liked him and he began to sing regularly and later introduced gags in between songs and eventually comedy took over and he became a top-of-the-bill comedian. His talent for making people laugh eventually took him all over the world appearing with cabaret stars from the UK and America including Frankie Howerd, Bob Monkhouse, Johnny Mathis, Ella Fitzgerald, Roy Orbison and Louis Armstrong on the international circuits of the UK, Africa, Australia, the Middle and Far East. However he never lost sight of his roots and always returned to the North East and in his own words said *"I'd rather work in the North-East than anywhere in the world."* Again in his own words he claimed to not having made any money. *"I blew it all on women, racing, smoking and drinking – and the rest I must have wasted"* he joked.

Having appeared on stage together on many occasions including charity fund raising events Brian Leonard and Bobby became good friends. After the comedian and magician Tommy Cooper collapsed and died in front of millions of TV viewers during the variety show Live from Her Majesty's in April 1984 Bobby Knoxall was invited to carry out Tommy's remaining contractual engagements – one of which was a week's appearance at the Fiesta Club in Stockton on Tees. Bobby contacted Brian and asked him if he would back him for his customary sung intros/finales to which Brian readily agreed and was paid £150 for doing so. He was a guest at Brian's 40 years in show business celebration party in 1997 presenting him with a bottle of champagne. He was awarded an MBE in 2004 for his services to entertainment and charity and sadly passed away in July 2009 having suffered from liver and kidney problems.

A singer from South Shields called Tommy Duffy was also on Beverley Agency's books in those early years who impersonated Frankie Vaughan complete with cane and high kicks and Brian recollects that he told Bobby Knoxall that he too was going to follow in his footsteps and take up comedy. Furthermore he told him that he was going to 'nick some of his act!' Bobby told him that if he could do it as good as him he could have it. Well he did and launched himself as Alan Fox and 'Foxy' became one of the best of the North East comics with a nationwide reputation as the 'Clean Comedian'.

Beverley also managed Julian Jorg the tenor referred to in Brian's recollections of his time in South Africa. In May 2013 Bill Reeves got in touch with Brian and went to see him perform at The Ship in Monkseaton where he told Brian that Julian had stayed with him for a few weeks. Knowing that he was dying he told Bill that he wanted to return to Australia where he had been so successful and asked if he could arrange it. Bill did so and Julian worked there in cabaret for 3 weeks and died during a performance.

Brian remained with Bill Reeves and the Beverley Agency for most of his career but had a big fall-out with Bart Elliott who had joined the agency from the Top Class agency. He decided to join the Round The Clock agency in Wallsend where he stayed for a couple of years before linking up with Hughie & Ian Turner and George MacLean at the Wansbeck Agency in Bedlington where Hughie's son Ian managed Brian for a few years. He subsequently joined Mark Lewis and Ronnie Vaughan at their Lewis Vaughan agency only to join up with Ian Simons and George MacLean at the Personal Management agency in Jarrow where he remained until he retired from clubland when he was 60 years old.

40 Years in the business

Brian's wife along with family members and friends decided to organise a surprise party to celebrate his forty years in show business. With the help of George MacLean, his agent at that time, the Pioneer Club at Annitsford was booked for a Thursday night and George contacted friends and people Brian had worked with over the years and invited them to attend. Helen set about catering for some 300 people and Brian remembers getting up on the morning of the 'do' to fabulous smells emanating from the kitchen and found her baking pies, sausage rolls and other delicacies for a buffet. When questioned she fibbed and told him it was for his nephew's 21st birthday party and he consequently never gave it another thought. Early that evening George MacLean and Brian's friend the priest Father Richard Harriott of St John the Baptist Roman Catholic Church Annitsford came to pick him up as they usually did on a Thursday evening to go to Andy Muat's house in Gosforth to play snooker and have a drink. On the way Father Harriott asked Brian if he minded them calling at the Pioneer Club in Annitsford as a good friend of his was celebrating a special birthday there and he had a bottle of whisky for him. Brian told him it wasn't a problem and when they arrived Father Harriott asked Brian & George to join him to meet the 'friend'.

When the door opened Brian was amazed to see all his family, friends and former colleagues as well as artistes he had worked with all sitting there and he instinctively turned to Father Harriott and exclaimed *"You bastard!"* *"Careful"* replied Father Richard *"I'm a Catholic priest you know ha ha..."* Brian immediately started bubbling and shed tears most of the night as he realised how many had turned up to help celebrate his 40 years in the business. Father Harriott addressed the gathering and thanked Brian, for although not a Catholic, he had raised a lot of money for the parish funds and had been a regular entertainer at the church's annual garden party. He commented *"Everyone is here because they want to share the night with their friend Vance Clayton"*.

Brian's first group *The Gators* were there - Brian & Will Pears, Dave Shipley, Ian Watson, Jim Hall and Mickey Lant along with Bobby Knoxall, Alan Snell, Larry Mason, Terry Milligan, John Garrimore, Al Meechie, Walter Gee and Johnny Hammond had travelled from Southport to be there. Former drummers and guitarists from the Vance Clayton eras - Keith Patterson, Dougie Windsor, John Siddle, Billy Lane, Mick Nicholson, Andy Muat, Keith Middleton and Neil Dixon aka Alvis Broon (a send-up of Elvis Presley). Former agents Bill Reeves, Bob Gladwin, Ralph Phillips, Ronnie Vaughan and Mark Lewis also attended along with former Butlins Redcoats with whom Brian had kept in touch.

Paul Squires from *The Millionaires* was scheduled to compere the show in a 'This Is Your Life' format but got a last minute booking on a cruise ship and was ably substituted by another great North East comedian Brian Lewis. He did a fabulous job and had everyone falling about. Brian Leonard was especially pleased to see his old pal from Dudley & Weetslade Club, their concert chairman Edgar Robinson and also Robson Green Snr. His son Robson Green Jnr. of course went on to become an actor, singer and TV presenter. Helen's buffet was its customary wonderful success and the entertainment was non-stop with various acts getting on stage to sing, play or perform comedy routines. These included Cindy Kelly, Dave and Carole Watson, Alvis Broon and Walter Gee & Frankie from Linseed and Aniseed who did a great version of the mime Old McDonald's Farm and the Mel Blanc classic 'I Taut I Taw A Puddy Tat' (I thought I saw a pussy cat) which brought the house down. The night finished off with Brian & Davey Herron performing as the *Vance Clayton Duo*.

Retirement from full time entertaining

By the age of 60 Brian had thought long and hard and eventually decided to finish with the clubs and he and Helen having for a while fancied buying a holiday home decided on a static caravan at Percy Wood Golf and Country Retreat in Swarland some six miles south of Alnwick in Northumberland. After the first couple of years which they had greatly enjoyed they decided to sell their house in Cramlington and upgrade their caravan as they wanted to retire there. They made many friends on the site including Les Foggin, their next door neighbour who helped Brian get into computers and did all his electrical jobs for him. Keith & Linda Thompson and Malcolm & Sylvia Rodham also became friends and when Malcolm left the site Brian purchased his golf buggy which he & Helen used to transport themselves from their caravan to the club house as well as for Brian's golfing days out.

Brian also became friends with the golf club steward Mel Harmison and his nephew Steven Harmison, the England and Durham cricketer, who bought a log cabin next door to him and Helen. Little Maureen Bagley was a close neighbour and friend too and Brian met another couple called Stu & Ros MacLean. Stu was a singer and asked Brian to help him put together a recording of the mining tribute song Working Man on a CD which he sold for charity and made a good sum of money. Another friend of Brian called Peter Leggate, a singer also known in club land as Darren Peters, visited him and Helen and commented what a fabulous place they had and he thought his wife would love to live there too. He took Sheila his wife up to view the whole set up and she immediately sold her house and they both moved to Percy Wood and remain there to this day.

In April 2012 Brian celebrated his 'three score years and ten' by jointly hosting a birthday party with his wife Helen – who was 65 on 20th April – in Shankhouse Central Working Men's Social Club in Cramlington. Some 300 people attended including family, friends and a host of entertainers that Brian had worked with over the years many of whom got up to perform as a tribute to him.

Ten years after retiring to Percy Wood they decided to sell up and return to Cramlington where they live in their cottage.

The Wedding Singer

The 2nd August 2013 was a special day for Brian & Helen when their eldest son Tony's daughter Ashley married Nigel Heron a Sergeant in the Scots Guards. Granddaughter Ashley had asked her granddad to be her wedding singer and although he readily agreed it has to be said it was with some apprehension knowing what an emotional day it would be for all concerned.

The wedding ceremony took place in St Agatha's Church at Easby Abbey or the Abbey of St Agatha which is an abandoned abbey on the eastern bank of the River Swale on the outskirts of Richmond in North Yorkshire and proved to be a wonderful setting for the wedding.

The reception for some 150 guests was held in the Sergeant's mess at Catterick Garrison where the Scots Guards have been based since 2008. The army prepared the meal although Helen made her granddaughter's wedding cake. Ashley had given her granddad a playlist of songs she wanted him to perform during the course of the day including those of Frank Sinatra & Michael Bublé. The bride, herself an accomplished singer, sang the appropriately worded 'Songbird' by Eva Cassidy to her groom and later duetted with her granddad. Brian had for some time prior to the wedding been trying to persuade son Tony to sing the beautiful ballad by the American Country group *Heartland* and called 'I Loved Her First' in which the narrator is talking to the man who is going to marry his daughter and about how difficult it is to do because he *loved her first*. However Tony understandably declined and his father, after a few weeks of rehearsing and full of emotion, did the honours!

Towards the end of the proceedings Brian got Tony, Ashley and her brother Harry up to jointly sing and play – 3 generations of the Leonard family 'on stage' together!

The Show Goes On

The *Vance Clayton Duo* had, as previously stated, also been the Sunday night resident band for ballroom dancing followers at The Benedictine Club in Cramlington until just a few years ago and as a result of a change in the pub management at their Tuesday night spot at The Ship in Monkseaton that came to end on 19th November 2013 when Brian & Davey Herron played to a packed lounge bar for the last time in a gig entitled *"The Day the Music Died"*.

Brian continues to perform with Davey as the *Vance Clayton Duo* for private functions including regular weekly sessions at The Seahorse public house in Blyth on a Wednesday evening when they play and sing popular ballads and invite members of the audience on stage to sing as well as hosting a music-cum-general knowledge quiz. The highlight of the evening occurs when Brian & Davey liven things up with dance music and the dancers among the audience including the Wednesday night 'girls' grace the dance floor *bopping and jiving* and everyone has a great time. Brian brings the evening to a close when he calls *'cuddly bums'* time at about 11:15 pm and sings either Eric Clapton's 'Wonderful Tonight' or 'The Answer to Everything' recorded by numerous artistes but originally Del Shannon.